Ideas for Teachers
Emergency!
A Book For
ALL Teachers

Virginia Ferguson
Peter Durkin

Longman Cheshire

Longman Cheshire Pty Limited
Longman House
Kings Gardens
95 Coventry Street
Melbourne 3205 Australia

Offices in Sydney, Brisbane, Adelaide
and Perth. Associated companies,
branches, and representatives
throughout the world.

Designed by Noniann Cabouret Lier
Illustrated by Rebecca Pannell and Maryann Hurley
Set in 10/12 pt Zapf Book Light (Linotron)
Produced by Longman Cheshire Pty Limited
Printed in Hong Kong

National Library of Australia
Cataloguing-in-Publication data

Ferguson, Virginia.
    Emergency!: a book for all teachers.

    Includes index.
    ISBN 0 582 66784 4.

    1. Activity programs in education. 2. Creative
activities and seat work. 3. Education, Elementary. I.
Durkin, Peter. II. Title.

372.13

Guide to grade levels:
J Junior
M Middle
U Upper

Contents

Acknowledgements

We are grateful to the following for permission to reproduce copyright material.

Associated Book Publishers (U.K.) Ltd, London for the story 'The Thin King and the Fat Cook' by Donald Bisset from *Time and Again Stories* published by Methuen Children's Books; Adam and Charles Black (Publishers) Limited, London for the poem 'The Bogeyman' by J. Prelutsky from *Nightmares*; The Bodley Head, London for 'The King Who Wanted to Touch the Moon', a West Indian Folk Tale chosen and edited by Norah Montgomerie in *More Stories to Read and to Tell*; Isobel Kendall Bowden for her poem 'Bushrangers' from *A First Australian Poetry Book* published by Oxford University Press Australia; Burke Publishing Company Limited, London for the poem 'Mud' by John Smith from *My Kind of Verse*; Curtis Brown (Aust.) Pty Ltd, Sydney for the story 'J. Roodie' by Robin Klein from *Ratbags and Rascals* published by J.M. Dent; Jonathan Cape Ltd, London for the poems 'Spaghetti' and 'The Little Blue Engine' by Shel Silverstein from *Where the Sidewalk Ends* © 1974 Snake Eye Music, Inc; E.P. Dutton, New York for the poem 'Jump or Jiggle' by Evelyn Beyer from *Another Here and Now Story Book* by Lucy Sprague Mitchell* © 1937 E.P. Dutton, renewed 1965 Lucy Sprague Mitchell; Faber and Faber Ltd, London for 'The Story of Eight People and Horace' by Alice M. Coats from *The Story of Horace*; Aileen Fisher for her poem 'Noses' from *Up the Windy Hill* published by Scott Foresman & Co; Fontana Paperbacks, London for the poem 'Dad and the Cat and the Tree' by Kit Wright from *Rabbiting on*; Harper & Row, Publishers, Inc New York for the poem 'All About Boys and Girls' by John Ciardi from *You Read to Me, I'll Read to You* published by J.B. Lippincott Co © 1962 John Ciardi; William Heinemann Ltd, London for the poem 'Holes of Green' by Aileen Fisher from *In the Woods, in the Meadow, in the Sky*; David Higham Associates Limited, London for the poem 'Cat' by Eleanor Farjeon from *Silver Sand and Snow* published by Michael Joseph; Laura Cecil, Literary Agent, London on behalf of the Author's Estate for the poems 'Mr Tom Narrow' and 'A Pig Tale' by James Reeves from *James Reeves The Complete Poems* published by William Heinemann Ltd © James Reeves Estate; Little, Brown & Co, Boston for the poem 'Bananas and Cream' by David McCord from *One at a Time* © David McCord; Thomas Nelson Australia, Melbourne for the poem 'Dead Man's Blood' by Peter Bradbury from *Twenty Treasure Chests*; Oxford University Press Canada, Ontario for the story 'The Princess of Tomboso' by Natalie Savage Carlson from *The Golden Phoenix and Other Fairy Tales from Quebec* by Marius Barbeau retold by Michael Hornyansky, © 1980 Oxford University Press; Penguin Books Ltd London for the poems 'If you hold a shell to your ear' by Max Fatchen from *Songs for My Dog and Other People* (Kestrel Books), © 1980 Max Fatchen and 'How to Treat the House Plants' by Kit Wright from *Hot Dog and Other Poems* (Kestrel Books), © 1981 Kit Wright and 'Who's been at the toothpaste?' by Michael Rosen from *You Tell Me* by Roger McGough and Michael Rosen (Kestrel Books), Michael Rosen poems © 1979 Michael Rosen, this collection © 1979 Penguin Books Ltd; Penguin Books Australia Ltd, Melbourne for the poem 'Car Attack' by Doug MacLeod from *In the Garden of Bad Things*; Routledge & Kegan Paul PLC, London for the poem 'Feather or Fur' by John Becker from *New Feather for an Old Goose*; Scholastic Inc, New York for 'A Hungry Story' by Ruth Belov Gross from *The Laugh Book* © 1971 Ruth Belov Gross; William Jay Smith for his poems 'Over and Under', 'Laughing Time' and 'Things' from *Laughing Time: Nonsense Poems* published by Delacorte Press 1980, © 1955, 1957, 1980 William Jay Smith; Viking Penguin Inc, New York for the poem 'Yellow Butter' by Mary Ann Hoberman from *Yellow Butter Purple Jelly Red Jam Black Bread* © 1981 Mary Ann Hoberman.

While every effort has been made to trace and acknowledge copyright, in some cases copyright proved untraceable. Should any infringement have occurred, the publishers tender their apologies.

1 Sure Fire Successes:

Thirty Activities That Always Work

We have described thirty sure fire successes here because that's how many we know of which really *are* sure fire successes. The activities are not arranged in any particular order. You can dip into them at random. Your selection will be determined by your own sense of urgency, the children's mood, or the current topic under discussion.

1   Word Guess: The Synonym Game
ORAL LANGUAGE   J M U

Two children stand at the front of the room with their backs to the chalkboard. The teacher writes a word, e.g. F L O W E R, on the board, so that all children except the two at the front can see.

The children in the grade then take it in turns to give clues about the word. The clues should be single word synonyms — in this case, *plant, rose, grows, petals, spring, perfume, garden . . .*
(For younger children, or even for some older classes, we often allow more than one word, or even a whole sentence — e.g. *It grows in the garden. It smells beautiful.*)

The two at the front make guesses based on the clues given. They do not take it in turns to answer — it is a race to find out who will be first to guess.

If a child guesses a word correctly, she is the winner and stays out the front, whilst the other child is replaced by the one who gave the clue which resulted in the correct guess. A new word is then written on the board, (children can be selected to do this) and a new game begins. The game can reach a frenetic pitch when the guesses are flying thick and fast. You can decide whether to let chaos reign, or to conduct a more sedate turn-by-turn game.

Needless to say the children prefer the former!

2   One Match, or One Minute Talks
ORAL LANGUAGE   J M U
WRITTEN LANGUAGE

Choose a topic from the list below, make up your own, or let the children compile a list. Give the children a number each (Sally is number 1, Ray is number 2 . . .) When their number is drawn they must talk for one minute on the topic chosen.

One brave teacher at Rosevern lights a match, announces the topic, and the speaker must conclude when the match burns out. It is probably safer to use a watch, but the match is so much more dramatic.

The time is so short that this is not a threatening oral activity for children; in fact some resent the limited time.

Choose all kinds of topics — broad, simple, funny, serious . . .

Some examples might be:

Carrots	Adults
Time	Hair
Yesterday	Luck
Buttons and bows	Trains
Boots and shoes	Fractions
Telling tales	Curls
It's not fair!	Crusts
Boring	People who borrow
Birthdays	Noses
Anger	T.V.
Going to bed	Time
Getting up	Waiting
Fear	Trouble
Afternoon tea	Wishes
When I grow up	Laughing
If I were mum	Spelling
Teachers	Saying goodbye

Variation
You can use these same topics as a **writing** activity. Say to the class, "I have written eight (or twelve or twenty-two) topics on the board.

I want you to think for two minutes and then write as much as you can on the topic you have chosen. You have exactly twenty-eight minutes."

3 Heads Down, Thumbs Up
LISTENING   J M U
DEVELOPING THE SENSES
HONESTY

We can't work out why, but this game is universally popular at all year levels — from Preps to Year 8. To succeed it depends totally on the participants' honesty. Yet in all the years we have been playing it, not one child has tried to cheat when his or her name has been called.

Five (or so) children are out the front of the class. The rest of the children are seated with heads on tables or desks, eyes closed, and one hand extended above head, elbow resting on the table and thumb pointing upwards. The five sneak around the room, selecting a thumb to tug, tap, touch, tip or flick. The sneakers then tiptoe to the front and ask those whose thumbs were chosen to guess who touched them.

A correct guesser then replaces the sneaker who touched him. Sneakers who are undetected remain out the front, and so the game continues . . . ad infinitum!

How do the children guess who touched them? Some listen for the foot-steps, others concentrate on the thumb tap itself, and almost all children subject the tapper to an inquisitional stare before making a guess. If you're game, try putting your own head down — it's an interesting experience.

4 Strip Tease
VISUAL DISCRIMINATION   J M U

One child is chosen to leave the room and make a minor alteration to his or her clothing — e.g. undo a button, pull a sleeve down a tiny way, take out one ear-ring, change a cuff, put watch or bangle on the other wrist, pull a hair out (they guess this one every time!).

The child who guesses correctly then has a turn as the strip tease. Beware if you do this with younger children. Their changes are far less discreet. One little boy returned to the room wearing only his singlet. The next one came clad only in a skimpy petticoat.

The game was promptly changed!

Variation

Blindfold
DEVELOPING THE SENSES   J M U

One teacher at Rosevern had a blind boy in her grade. Now and then the others teased him. Just to let them know what it was like, we would blindfold some of them for a few minutes. Their reactions to the experience prompted much discussion and greater understanding. As a result we played a number of other games which developed into sure fire successes:

* Blindfold a child, choose an object from the room which can be seen by all the others. Let the blindfolded child touch the object and try to guess what it is.

* Hold up an object for all except the blindfolded child to see. Ask the grade to describe the object without naming it. The blindfolded child has to guess the object. The next one blindfolded is the one who gave the winning clue.

* Work in pairs. One child is blindfolded, the other is his guide. The guide has to direct the blindfolded child to a certain point, by giving explicit instructions. Later, they swap roles and return to the classroom to discuss their reactions with the whole grade.

5 Concentration
VISUAL DISCRIMINATION   J M U
OBSERVATION
CLASSIFICATION
MEMORY

A major advantage of this activity is that it can be adapted to many situations and subject areas. It is basically a memory game in which the children turn cards over in an attempt to find pairs.

Playing cards are ideal for this activity. All the cards are placed face down on the table or floor. The children take turns to turn up a card. When all children playing have seen the card the same player turns up another card. If a player turns up a pair — i.e. two tens or two kings, he keeps the cards. If not, it is the next player's turn. To get a pair the players must try to remember which cards have been turned over so that they can make a match when it is their turn.

Variations
Flash cards for spelling, tables, basic words, equations, four processes, phrases etc. can be used.

For the upper grades intricate designs, photos, pictures might be matched.

On a wet day you might ask the children to actually make some concentration cards. You supply uniformly cut white card.

From two to about ten children can play this game, and it can be modified to suit Preps as well as older children.

6 Switch Around
VISUAL DISCRIMINATION   M U
MEMORY

One of the simplest activities, this memory game is unceasingly popular. To begin, one child is chosen to stand with her back to the class. Another child, unseen by the one in front, is chosen to leave the classroom.

The children then all change places, and the child at the front turns around and tries to identify the one who is out of the room.

Change guessers and time their efforts. Who is quickest? This activity is (mostly) unsuitable for young children (Preps-Grade 2). They are too egocentric, and are rarely able to guess who is missing. If clues are given, the game is made easier, and some of our Grades 1 and 2 enjoy playing it. Clues: "It's a girl." Child guesses, and if not successful, another clue is added. "She's a girl with long dark hair." If unsuccessful again, add another clue. "She's a girl with long dark hair and she is a fast runner." If they haven't guessed after three clues, they are out.

7 Name — Game — Fame
ORAL LANGUAGE   M U
GENERAL KNOWLEDGE
CLASSIFICATION

To participate successfully in this activity, you must have quick wits, good co-ordination *and* a knowledge of specific subjects, e.g.
NAME: any place or person's name
GAME: any sport or game
FAME: anything or anyone famous

Make a ball out of crumpled paper. One child comes out the front and throws the crumpled paper ball to another child in the grade. At the same time she calls out one of the three categories — i.e. NAME, GAME or FAME. The child who catches the ball must name something in the category, and then she must throw the ball to someone else **at the same time calling out a new category**.

It is amazing how difficult this last part is. Most children become so excited that they call out the category asked, but throw the ball to a new person, quite forgetting to shout out a new category.

Try different categories —
NOUNS — VERBS — ADJECTIVES
ANIMAL — VEGETABLE — MINERAL
TABLES
SPELLING
FISH — BIRDS — INSECTS

---

8   Memory Tray
MEMORY   M U

Use materials from your emergency bag of tricks (see page 185) for this activity. Display twelve different objects on a tray. Show the tray for about 45 seconds, then cover it up. Give the children five minutes to recall as many articles as they can.

There are many **variations** on the memory idea. One that we have found highly successful is to read a poem like *Dead Man's Blood* to test the children's memory and understanding.

Dead Man's Blood

Boat, map, anchor, land;
Feet, boots, mud, sand —

Pack, load, tie, mules;
Picks, hatchets, shovels, tools —

Jungle, logs, vines, trees;
Creeks, bushes, bugs, bees —

X, dig, tension, stare;
Strike, metal, uncover, bare —

Look, greed, hunger, cry;
Loud, scream, murder, die —

Cut, slash, strangle, brawl;
Mutilate, howl, mangle, maul . . .

Silence, twitch, none, mud;
Jewels, treasure, DEAD MAN'S BLOOD!

Peter Bradbury

Read the poem once, then ask the children to tell you as many words as they can remember. Then say, "Now I will read the poem a second time and I want you to really try very hard to remember even more words."

You will be surprised at their recall. As they guess a word, we place a soft line under or through the word guessed. In most cases nearly every word is recalled. We then ask them to tell us the story behind the poem. This can be a written activity, but the shared oral experience is very satisfying for both the teacher and the children.

---

9   Four Questions
ORAL LANGUAGE   J M U
WRITTEN LANGUAGE

This is an activity for children who can write. Do it orally with little children.

Say to the group: "Write down four questions which you have often thought about, or which you would like answered." They can be any kind of question — factual, philosophical (we usually try to explain that term — What is Life?), flippant, fantastic, fatal, — or ordinary.

"Will you answer them?" a young cynic once asked. We replied that we'd do our best. "Well, I've only got a few: Is religion true? Why are we here, and what's life all about?"

Needless to say, dozens of discussions, arguments, debates, opinions and library research activities could follow *Four Questions*. Here are some examples from Grades 5 and 6:

Where did God come from?
Why do birds eat worms?
Why are people people?
Why do people born in China have a Chinese accent?
Is there an after-life, and will it ever fill up?
I would like to know why some people think daydreaming is silly, and why people can't understand how nice it is to read.
Is Atlantis true?
Will there be a war called the Last War?

Anonumous, after some cajoling, was quietly satisfied to allow his work to be used here:

Give the children a sheet of paper and ask them to write as quickly as possible, without stopping at all, for a specified period. They can write about anything which comes into their heads — it's really a modified form of stream-of-consciousness writing.

If they can't think of anything, they write, "I am in our room and I can't think of anything to write. Everyone else is writing. Elke has written five lines, but she is smart. I wish I was . . . . . "

This is an effective method for overcoming the Fright-to-Write syndrome. Children are under no obligation to show the work to their teachers. Mostly they tear their pages up. Occasionally we plead to read their efforts, promising to throw out any marked DESTROY, or return those to children who wish to keep their pages.

to write and while my blue catches its breath it ahh it seems as though its working again, it got its breath back its spitting out ink at just the word write face but my hand still feels though it will burst yes I think that my head is in for the worst. Now Percy my brain is exorsted its feeling worse, worse than before but yet I will write some more I hope you don't mind if its more junk than before but thats the way it goes or as some say thats the way the cookie crumbles, crumbles all away brocken into tiny bits, itsi witsi witsi bits its brocken all apart now what will I eat for deasent. What I am writing is not a poem not a story I hope the mistakes don't bother you cause if I read this I prefere my head down a loo. This story no poem no rym no no I dont know what to call it though I could call it a gut reaction I could call it a piece of rubbish but its to good for that or is it that you know I should learn short hand and I could write this quiker

Anonumous

6

11 Here is the Answer: What is the Question?
LATERAL THINKING   U

This is a problem solving activity. The answer is twenty-eight. Write down at least eight questions to which the answer is twenty-eight.

E.g.
  i   14 + 14 =
  ii How many would there have been at The Last Supper if there had been 15 more?
  iii 28 + (28 × 0) + 46 − 46 =
  iv What happened when twenty boys sat down to eat?
  v   What is the number shown in this mirror?

  vi 8 2
  vii Two and one-third cricket teams.
  viii What month has this many days except in every fourth year?
  ix That many blackbirds plus four more.

Other answers could be:

Fish and chips	Jelly
Friends	Poems
The moon	Sneeze
A smile	Worm
Kookaburra	Pyjamas

At first children and adults find this difficult, but it only takes practice. Do a few examples with the whole class first. Their questions must be so exact that no other answer is possible. For example, if someone wrote as the question for *Moon* — "What is something up in the sky at night?" — that is not specific enough. Stars, planets, UFOs could also apply.

There will always be several correct questions, and very few children will write the same thing.

Here are some likely answers to
The answer is moon: What is the question?

What did the nursery rhyme cow jump over?

"By the light of the silvery . . . ."

What did Neil Armstrong step on before any other man?

What reflects the light of the sun at night?

What is a four letter word which rhymes with *spoon*, and starts with M? Hint — sky.

What is sometimes new, sometimes full, sometimes half, but never old?

12 Character — Time — Place — Event
ORAL EXPRESSION   M U
WRITTEN EXPRESSION

This activity requires some preparation, but the effort is worth it. Make four sets of cards from the lists below. Use a different colour for each category — e.g. pink for character, blue for time, yellow for place and grey for event.

Ask the children to help you make the cards. Once they are made, you can use them over and over again.

Character

a lonely giant
Prince Charles
two pretty models
a school Principal
an ugly princess
a pale-faced miser
a footsore swagman
a caged bird
Man Friday
a lost spaceman
a funny farmer
six dwarves

Time

at the crack of dawn
as the cock crowed
just before midnight

when the bell tolled
after dark
at $\frac{1}{4}$ to 1
when the alarm rang
as the sun reached its peak
when the owl hooted
at dinner-time
2020 A.D.
some time

Place

behind the old bark hut
under the haystack
in the desert
a haunted cowshed
a deserted rubbish tip
in a T.V. studio
in a demonstration
high rise flats
the Hilton hotel
deeper and deeper towards the centre
beside a log fire
near the pig sty

Event

something dreadful happened
there was a loud explosion!
the plane crashed
they had champagne for breakfast
it went on and on
they simply couldn't believe it
they broke down and wept
they shook hands
it was a miracle!
pandemonium broke loose
he/they had to run away
tears filled their eyes

The children work in groups of four. Give each group four cards — one from each group. Then ask them to make a story incorporating what is written on each card. The cards are merely the skeleton for the story. — children are expected to add details; to fill out the story. They may later tell or perform their story for the class.

For written expression, each child is given his own set of four cards. This is a helpful exercise for children who are not confident about writing, or who constantly regurgitate what they saw on T.V. last night. The cards give them security — they have a starting point, and may continue to write with confidence.

---

13   **Pick the Nursery Rhyme**
      LISTENING   J M U
      RHYTHM

All children love nursery rhymes, and the rhythm is unmistakeable. To begin, the teacher should tap out the rhythm of a nursery rhyme by clapping her hands together, or by using chime bars, drums or rhythm sticks. The rest of the grade tries to detect which nursery rhyme is being played.
   When the rhyme is discovered, the child who identified it first is the new leader.
   Often — particularly with younger children — the whole grade will want to sing along with the rhyme after it has been discovered. Encourage them to sing, with leader beating in rhythm, before going on with the next rhyme.

---

14   **Follow These Words**
      ORAL EXPRESSION   J M U
      DRAMA
      MEMORY
      FOLLOWING INSTRUCTIONS

Some children find this activity difficult. They have to absorb instructions to complete differing activities in sequence. The instructions vary in complexity according to the grade levels. Invent your own instructions, or ask the children to help.

Examples for the junior grades:
   Find something red, give it to a friend, then

smile at everyone.

Sit down, stand up, sit down again and spin around twice.

Examples for the middle grades:

Stand on one foot, clap your hands three times, then run to the chalkboard and write your name in blue chalk.

Say the ABC, count to ten, name three green things, then skip to the door.

Examples for upper grades:

Walk to the chalk board, draw four chooks and three eggs, turn around five times, say a rhyme for table and spell champagne.

Draw an upside down hut with a cat near the back door, a rooster on the roof, and three clouds in the sky.

---

15 Whisper a Message
LISTENING   J M U
CLEAR DICTION

Children form a circle, seated on the floor. The teacher writes a message on a piece of paper and gives it to Child Number One, who then whispers the same message to the next child — and so on, all around the ring. When the circle is completed, the last child stands up and loudly repeats the message. Very rarely are the messages the same, especially if you choose tricky tongue tanglers:

Pre-shrunk shirts shouldn't shrink in the suds.

Blame Peggy Babcock for the blemish on the big black book.

Throw three frisbees, Theo — quickly — don't daydream or dawdle.

With young children you could whisper the sentence to the first child. Invent easier examples.

---

16 The Quickest Clown
DRAMA   J M U
MOVEMENT

Read the verse to the children, asking them to think up suitable actions. Ask for suggestions; accept those that are the same as yours.

The quickest clown came to town.	
It was no surprise when he rolled his eyes.	*Children roll eyes.*
His face was red as he rubbed his head.	*Children rub heads, and keep rolling eyes.*
And he looked so glum as he patted his tum.	*Children pat tums, and keep on rubbing heads and rolling eyes.*
He cried, "Oh heck!" as he twisted his neck.	*Children turn necks from left to right, whilst continuing all other actions.*
He tapped one shoe and we did too.	*Children tap shoes, whilst continuing all previous actions.*
He kept bobbing to the ground without any sound.	*Children bob up and down, whilst continuing all previous actions.*
Then he quickly said, "I'm off to bed!"	*Children cease all actions, and flop to the floor, asleep. Silence prevails.*

---

17 The Lion Hunt
DRAMA   J M U
MOVEMENT

This poor lion! Never has there been such a hunted creature. Many teachers will know this tried and true action story, but there have been many alterations and variations. When you first try this activity with a grade, you will need to demonstrate the action and sounds. On subsequent occasions, the children will do the acting with no prompting at all. However, it is probably better if you lead the actions and sounds each time. Sometimes the children get quite carried away by the excitement. Say to your class of intrepid hunters: Today, we're going on a lion hunt. What will we need?

Chn: will respond with various answers — guns, net, hat, lunch, drink.

Tchr: Are you ready?

Chn: Y E S!

Tchr: Well, hurry along — kiss Mum goodbye.

Chn: S l u r p. (*Make a slurpy kissy noise — you join in.*)

Tchr: Now, down the path, and open the creaky gate.

Chn: C — r — e — a — k . . . (*Make a creaky noise from the back of the throat.*)

Tchr: Let's walk briskly along. (*Clap hands briskly on thighs.*)

Chn: (*Clap hands briskly on thighs.*)

Tchr: I think you can go a bit faster.

Chn: (*Faster clapping of hands on thighs.*)

Tchr: Here's a bridge — be careful!

Chn: (*Make bonketty fist noises on chest.*)

Tchr: Whatever next? Look at all this muddy slushy ground!

Chn: (*Make slushy slurpy noises as they paddle through.*)

Tchr: At last — some good luck! Here are some horses. Hop on, everyone. Cling tight!

Chn: (*Clip-clop noises — some with tongue clicking, others with gallopy, rhythmic clapping.*)

Tchr: We must dismount here. Tie up the horses and get ready to jump this creek. Hurry up now! Run! Run faster!
(Make sure the children are following your actions as you will have to show them when — and how — to jump this creek!)

Chn: (*Speedy clapping of hands on thighs, then a short P A U S E as they leap, then a loud clap as they land safely on the other side.*)

Tchr: Good! We're nearly there, but first we must climb this hill.

Chn: (*Puff and pant to the top.*)

Tchr: Phew! We're at the top. Have a drink, then we'll be off down the hill.

Chn: (*Take a gurgly swig of their pretend drink, then race down the hill, making vigorous clapping hands on thighs sounds.*)

Tchr: It's very dangerous to run down hills, but never mind . . . shhhh . . . I think the Lion's Cave is somewhere close by. (*Whisper*) Yes, I think it's just over there. Shhhh. Quietly tiptoe after me. (*Hold one arm high, and tiptoe with two fingers.*)

Chn: (*Copy teacher's tiptoe actions.*)

Tchr: Now, here's the cave. I think I can see two yellow eyes glaring at us. I think I can see some sharp long teeth! Quick — get out your guns — Ready — aim — FIRE!!

Chn: B A N G G G G G !!!!!

Tchr: (*Yelling*) YOU MISSED! Run for it! The lion's after us.
ROARRRRRR! ROARRRRR! ROARRRRR!

Chn: (*Will probably join in the frequent loud roars*)
(Now the actions are repeated in reverse order, at even greater speed, as the children race home.)

Tchr: Quick — up the hill.

Chn: (*Puff and pant.*)

Tchr: Here's that creek. Never mind about jumping — leap in and swim for your lives.

Lion: (*both children and teacher*) ROARRRRRRRRRRR!

Chn: (*Splishy splashy noises as they swim across the creek.*)

Tchr: Jump on the horses — quickly.

Chn: (*Same actions as before, but faster.*)

Tchr: Quickly — off the horses now, and get through this mud.

Chn: (*Make very quick slushy glushy slurpy muddy noises.*)

Tchr: Here's the bridge.

Lion: ROARRRR!

Chn: (*Bonketty fist noises on chest.*)

Tchr: Run, run!!

Chn: (*Clap hands on thighs at an awesome speed.*)

Tchr: Thank goodness, here's the gate.

Chn: (*Pitter-patter.*)

Tchr: Up the path.

Chn: C r e a k . . .

Tchr: (Panting) Kiss Mum.

Chn: (*Slurp a kiss, and pant.*)

Tchr: Well, thank goodness we beat that lion. Have a good sleep tonight, and tomorrow you can all write a story about *Our Lion Hunt.*

Chn: GRRRRRRRRR! (or m o a n and s i g h — if they're polite!)

Use your imagination to make new stories and sounds. We became so tired of that lion that we've held witch hunts, giant hunts, dragon hunts, pirate hunts, dinosaur hunts, snake hunts, Yeti hunts . . .

---

18 Miming
DRAMA   J M U

Of all these sure fire successes, this is the surest and the firiest!

You can do it two ways.

Ask the child to choose a number between one and eighty-eight, and he mimes the activity written beside that number.

Another (and better) way is to write each mime onto a small library card. Each child selects a card and presents his mime. One of our Grade 5's uses a table as a stage, and the children are presented as "Introducing Eliza Marceau" or "Marcel Regos".

The applause is deafening, and the requests for this activity never wane.

Most of these mimes would be too difficult for young children. We usually ask them to act out something of their own choice, or we suggest: "Act out something Mummy might do", "Turn yourself into an animal", "Show us some jobs you know about".

As for the older children, the child who first guesses what the actor is miming has the next turn.

Eighty-eight sure fire mimes

1 You are packing a suitcase, then trying to do up the catch. The case is very full and very heavy.

2 You are changing a baby's nappy.

3 You are trying to dress a toddler who keeps running away.

4 You are waiting and waiting to get served in a shop. Just as the assistant is about to serve you, someone else barges in and gets served first.

5 You are hitchhiking to Sydney, or Perth or Darwin or Launceston.

6 You find an old Aladdin-type lamp. You polish it frantically, think of a wish and — nothing happens!

7 You are trying to teach someone to knit.

8 You are flying a kite in a strong wind, and it gets caught in a tree.

9 You try to stifle a sneeze.

10 You are a mouse sniffing some cheese, and you get caught in a trap.

11 You are a pirate being made to walk the plank.

12 You are a cat washing yourself.

13 You are taking the garbage bag out, when it splits open and you fall in the mess.

14 You are a tightrope walker at a circus.

15 You are a famous pianist. Come on stage, perform, then take your bow.

16 You are walking across some stepping stones in a creek. You slip on one and fall in.

17 You are babysitting, and the baby won't stop bawling.

18 You are waiting at the airport to meet someone. You become anxious as hundreds of people have emerged — then suddenly your friend appears.

19 You are pleading with your parents: "Please may I take my girl/boyfriend out."

20 You are rowing in a canoe when your only oar is swept away. The current is swift, it's a freezing day — and you are not a good swimmer.

21 You are milking a cow.

22 You watch a plane as it crashes from the sky.

23 You are terrified of storms and a huge one blows up as you are walking home.

24 You are at a concert. Everyone is absorbed and silent, but you are absolutely bursting to cough.

25 A really starving explorer is invited to dinner in the desert.

26 Finally, after years of trying, you teach yourself to whistle.

27 A burglar, with a sackful of stolen goods, climbs through the window of the house he has robbed.

28 Climb a ladder to get a tennis ball down from the roof.

29 Take a football mark in slow motion (as shown on T.V.).

30 You are Baby Bear in *The Three Bears*. Mime the porridge, chair and bed scenes.

31 Make a snowman.

32 Be the wolf in *The Three Little Pigs*, huffing and puffing.

33 You go outside to take the cat and the milkbottles out — and find a baby on your doorstep.

34 Be a famous weight-lifter.

35 You are digging the garden when your spade strikes something metal.

36 You are a young child playing with your imaginary friend.

37 You are in the last lap of the marathon.

38 You are a scarecrow, or you *make* a scarecrow.

39 Be Old King Cole.

40 Be a teacher praising her young class for their beautiful behaviour.

41 You are fishing and you catch an old boot.

42 David and Goliath. You are David.

43 You are a child listening to an excellent storyteller, telling a sad story with a happy ending.

44 You are a princess who decides to throw her crown away.

45 You have a violent headache.

46 You are an insomniac — you count sheep, toss, turn and moan.

47 You are throwing confetti at a wedding.

48 You are an eccentric artist painting a vivid sunset.

49 You are a checkout person in a supermarket.

50 You are a model posing for Playboy magazine.

51 You are bitten by a snake.

52 You are trying to teach someone how to swim.

53 You are decorating a birthday cake or a Christmas tree.

54 You are hammering a nail and you miss, hitting your finger!

55 You are riding a bike for the first time.

56 You are Elvis Presley.

57 You are a lawyer in a court room.

58 You buy some jeans and pay for them with Bankcard.

59 A mother smacks her naughty child, then the father remonstrates with her for being cruel.

60 Unwrapping, with feverish excitement, a huge parcel.

61 You have a wonderful idea while you are in the bath.

62 You have to answer a knock at the door but you cannot see a thing without your glasses, and they're lost.

63 You are embarrassed because the person sitting next to you falls asleep during a

boring lecture. You try to wake him up.

64 You are a spider spinning a web.
65 You are a witch with her cat on a broomstick, shooting high in the sky.
66 You are a lion, a monkey and then a giraffe.
67 You sail away on a magic carpet.
68 Be the maid who was "pegging out the clothes, when down came a blackbird and pecked off her nose".
69 You are woken up by a very early morning phone call on the first day of your holidays.
70 The ceiling of your house falls down.
71 You scratch the black bits from a piece of burnt toast.
72 You are alone in the lounge room when you get the feeling that someone is peeping at you through the keyhole.
73 Cinderella scrubs the floors while her step-sisters get ready to go to the ball.
74 You are late out after being warned to be home early. You creep in, trying not to let your parents hear.
75 You pull a face, the wind changes, and you stay like it!
76 You are strolling along when all of a sudden you are solidified — turned into stone.
77 You are a windmill.
78 You beckon to a friend but she tells you to get lost.
79 You find a secret doorway in the passage of an old house.
80 You are a mean miser, counting his money.
81 You are chopping the head off a chook.
82 You are an adult — trying to teach a child to tell the time.
83 You are in trouble, but you try to blame it onto the person sitting next to you.
84 You watch the Tattslotto draw on T.V. — and you win!
85 You are chopping wood.
86 You hurt your leg and limp for a while. Your leg heals, but you keep limping (for sympathy). One day you limp on the wrong leg and you are caught out!

87 You are on a farm and walk right into a fresh wet cow-flop.
88 Your bike starts to fly.

19 Musical Detective
MUSIC PERCEPTION   J M U

Ideally, this activity should be played in a hall or a multi-purpose room, where the children have room to move, and where the music is loud. However, it is also posssible to play in the classroom without music.

With music

A detective is chosen to leave the room. In her absence, a leader is chosen whose job it is to lead the class in movement to music. The music may be chosen by you or the children — the only criterion is that it has a good beat.

Start the music and the leader begins a movement which the rest follow. She might tap her knee in time to the music, or throw her feet in the air (à la Mexican Hat Dance), or do the twist. Everyone else follows. The detective returns and has three guesses to discover who is the leader. The class does everything possible to keep the identity of the leader a secret. If the detective discovers the leader, the detective has another turn; if not, the leader becomes the detective, and so the game continues.

Other movements might be — click fingers, slap thighs, wiggle bottoms, nod head, swing arms . . .

Without music

This game is successful without recorded music. To play, the leader makes any kind of movement (as described above). Most children can follow the leader without looking directly at her — so the detective must become very adept to make a catch.

---

20 Statues
MUSIC   J M U
MOVEMENT

This can be done with or without music, although we prefer the former. The music can be very simple: a child tapping a xylophone, chime bars, maracas or rhythm sticks. When the beat begins, all the children move around the room in rhythmic response to the music. The instant the music stops, they must freeze like a statue. The teacher moves around, admiring the statues, peering into their eyes, waving a hand in front of their faces, telling jokes . . . Anyone who so much as moves a muscle is out. "What about breathin'?" we were asked, and so we conceded the point — breathing is tolerated.

The music begins again, and the game continues.

A variation, equally popular, and which does not need music, is *Haystacks*.

Variation

Haystacks
IMAGINATIVE PLAY   J M U

Say to the class, "Make yourself into a haystack!" We're at a loss to know how so many city children who have never heard of a haystack, let alone seen one, are able to make the most life-like haystacks. We have never once been asked, "What's a haystack?"

(As we were revising the first draft of this book, a VISION came to us: Nursery rhyme haystacks — such as the one under which Little Boy Blue is fast asleep . . .)

You can ask them to make themselves into ANYTHING: a capital B, a seven, an X, a bridge, lightning, a match (Nadia, a brunette in Grade 1 lamented, "I wish I had red hair". Then she quickly resolved the problem — "I know — I'm a *burnt* match!")

---

21 Grock Day Deeds
SCIENCE   J M U
ENVIRONMENTAL STUDIES
SOCIAL STUDIES

There are many variations of Grocking, but the one we prefer is an outdoor activity, similar to the old fashioned Scavenger Hunt.

Pin a large sheet of card to a tree or a fence, and then give the group a certain time (15–25 minutes) to collect and complete all the things listed.

Vary the tasks to suit the ages of the children, who work in pairs. You can modify this activity to suit a variety of themes or subjects being treated in the grade which you are teaching.

Again, you can vary it for a wet day. The things to be found will all be in the classroom, and can be discovered with minimum movement from the desk or table; e.g. a dictionary, a piece of chalk, a blue pencil, three red things, a rubber, a drawing pin . . .

Here is a list for an outdoor Grock day:
Grock day Deeds
1 Pick a piece of grass exactly 9.5 cm long.
2 Find a stone as big as a 20 cent piece.
3 Sketch a leaf from the second biggest tree in the yard.
4 Make a bark rubbing.
5 Find a feather.
6 Pick up a piece of litter.

7 Record the biggest and smallest living creature you see.

8 Measure in handspans the distance between the first branch of a tree and the ground.

9 Which tree is the best one to hug?

10 Estimate in metres the distance between this note and the nearest gate.

11 Sketch the position of the sun in relation to the trees and buildings nearby.

12 Stop for a minute or two to listen for sounds. Write down as many as you can remember.

22   Sock Puppet
DRAMA   J M U

Everyone knows how to make a simple sock puppet, but by using **two** socks, you can achieve far more interesting creations.

First you slip one sock on your hand, heel up. Place a wad of crushed tissue in the tip of the sock (i.e. past your fingers), then slip the second sock over the first.

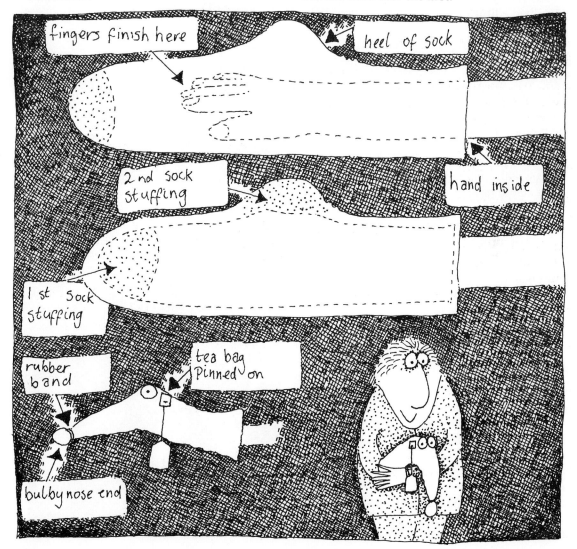

Place a rubber band tightly around the wad of tissue.

Pad the heel part of the outer sock with cotton wool, rags or tissues, so that it looks like the head of a Snoopy dog. Use round library-dot stickers for eyes, and use safety pins to pin on some ears. (We use tea-bags — they look funny.)

Hold your puppet over your other arm (as if he's leaning over a fence) and get him to tell some silly nursery rhymes — "Mary had a little . . . ummm . . " ("Yes?" you say encouragingly as he looks at you.) "Mary had a little — er — um hippopotamus . . ??"

Even if your best jokes fail, we can almost guarantee that this won't. Just tell a nursery rhyme, and get it wrong!

If you want to make different creatures, pad the sock differently: an elephant would have a much longer nose; a snake would be longer and hissier.

You could use the puppet to help younger children with their tables. Dog would get them wrong all the time, so that even the slowest children would feel superior and amused.

Older children could make puppets, and perhaps present a puppet play for younger children.

---

23 Shipwreck
PHYSICAL EDUCATION   J M U
LISTENING

It is most important to have clearly marked boundaries for this hectic activity: outdoors on a marked court, or in a hall or gym. A classroom — unless very large — is not suitable. The teacher is the Captain, whose warnings and orders must be obeyed by the crew.

When he shouts "Waves coming THIS way!" — pointing in a particular direction — the children must race off in the opposite direction. (This is usually accompanied by wild shrieks!)

He then shouts, "Waves coming THAT way!" and again, children must run in the opposite direction. He varies his directions, and when he calls, "Now the BOOM'S coming over!" all children must throw themselves onto the deck, to avoid being flattened.

Blissful silence then ensues.

The Captain can make other orders such as "Scrub the deck!" "Stand to attention and salute the Captain!" "Walk the plank!" Whenever things seem as if they're about to get out of control, call loudly, "Now the BOOM'S coming over!"

Variation
A quieter variation, also needing clearly marked boundaries, is **Octopus** described in the *Life Be In It New Games Booklet*.

16

Five or more children are chosen to be the Octopuses; the rest are the fish. The octopuses lie flat on their backs in the middle of the room (or court) waving their "tentacles" (arms and legs). The fish have to cross the room, past the octopuses, to the safety of the water on the far side. Any fish stung by the tentacles (i.e. touched) become octopuses and must lie down with the others.

Towards the end of the game there are many octopuses and a very few timid fish. That's when the Big Shark (the teacher) chases the fish through the octopuses. The game ends when there are no fish left.

24 Kickball
PHYSICAL EDUCATION   J M U

Kickball is a variation of continuous cricket, but it has the additional advantage of requiring less sophisticated physical skills. Therefore all the children can play it with confidence, and it can be adapted to suit any grade in the school.

The only equipment needed is a wicket (an old rubbish bin will do), a soft rubber ball (somewhat bigger than a tennis ball) and two markers. The children are divided into two teams: the Kickers and the Fielders. The kickers line up near the wicket, the fielders spread out to retrieve the ball, and should include a wicket-keeper.

The game begins when the bowler (who is one of the fielders, or for the junior grades, the teacher) bowls the ball under arm. The kicker tries to kick the ball as far as she can. To score, the kicker must run around a marker, placed some ten metres from the wicket, and then run back to the wicket. She must run whether she has kicked the ball or not.

The fielders must return the ball to the bowler who tries to hit the wicket before the kicker gets back. The kicker continues to score for as long as she can continue to kick the ball and run. The kicker is out if she is caught, or if the ball hits the wicket. All the children in the kicking side have a turn, and when they're all out, they change places with the fielding side.

25 Newcomb
PHYSICAL EDUCATION   M U

A variation on volleyball, Newcomb has been adapted to enable younger children to participate with some degree of success. You will need a light basketball, or a volleyball.

The age of the players decides the height of the net. Children in upper primary grades should play with the net at a height of almost two metres.

To begin, one member of a team standing on the back line throws the ball over the net. The opponents catch the ball and pass it back. The passing continues until the ball is dropped — then a point is awarded to the other team. The ball is then served from the other end, and the game continues. Each team serves alternately, and every point counts towards the team's total.

The ball can be caught by any player but it must not hit the ground. It can be passed forward from the back line to the players at the net so that they can throw it over the net to their team's advantage.

If the ball is thrown into the net or outside the lines, a point is lost.

Adapted from Curriculum Guide: *Physical Education for Primary Schools Book 4 — Ball Handling Skills and Games* (Education Department of Victoria, 1972).

(There are fifty other excellent ball games clearly described and illustrated in this book.)

26 Tables Races
MATHS   M U

There are many variations, but two of the most popular are the Pairs Table Race where there is one winner, and the Around the Room Tables Race where the whole grade wins.

For the **Pairs Table Race**, the grade is divided into two even groups, who then stand in two straight lines next to each other, making pairs. Tables are given to each pair orally by the teacher. The first child with the answer joins the end of his line, and the loser sits down. If the teams become unbalanced, they are rearranged evenly at intervals. The last eight children are considered to have reached the finals. The winner is the last person standing.

In the **Around the Room Tables Race**, the children try to beat the clock. Prior to beginning, the order of answering around the room is decided. At the word ''GO!'' the clock is started and the teacher asks the first child a table. The child answers, and if correct, she or he asks the second child another table. That child then asks the next child a table, and so on all around the room. If any child gets a table wrong, they have three guesses before the teacher tells them the correct answer. (This procedure causes a delay, and so extends the time taken by the grade to complete the game.)

The idea is for the children in the grade to beat their record. If their time at 9.30 was 3 minutes, 35 seconds, hopefully at 12.10 it will be less.

This game can be continued over a number of weeks, and can be adapted to incorporate number facts, spelling words . . . .

27 Buzzz
MATHS   J M U

This is one of the oldest games of the lot. You'll find it in the old pink Maths. *Curriculum Guide A* (Victorian Education Department — 1967), together with a number of excellent counting and maths games like *Old Tom*, *Greedy Eagle*, *Shooting Ducks*, *Skittles*, and *Apple Tree*.

For Preps, Buzz is really only an elimination game. The children stand in a circle and count from one to ten. The child whose turn it is to say *ten* also says *BUZZZ*, and sits. The next child commences again at one, and so the game continues until there is one child — the winner — left standing.

For children in the middle and upper grades, there are many variations. For example, in *BUZZZ with nines*, the children count, but any number which has anything to do with nine must be substituted by the word BUZZZ. e.g. 1, 2, 3, 4, 5, 6, 7, 8, BUZZZ, 10, 11, 12, 13, 14, 15, 16, 17, BUZZZ, BUZZZ, 20, 21, 22, 23, 24, 25, 26, BUZZZ, 28, BUZZZ ....

You can go to 100, and then come back to zero. Of course you could use any number.

---

28   Race to Find the Sentence
LISTENING   M U
READING
LOCATIONAL SKILLS

Give each child a copy of the same book. (The old Grade Readers are a wonderful resource.) Then read out several sentences from the book, and the race is on to see who can find the sentence first. This is an excellent activity for teaching the children such skills as skimming, recognition of different styles of writing, and the use of contents and index.

If you can't provide the whole class with the same title, give equal sized groups sets of identical books and choose several sentences from each.

Variations
Variations of this activity which never fail to get the children racing are:
   Race to find a word . . . using dictionaries
   Race to find a town, city, country, river
   . . . using an Atlas
   Race to find a name . . . using a telephone book

Race to find a street . . . using a directory
The variations are only limited by the number of copies of a particular book available.

---

29   The Team Picks the Word
READING COMPREHENSION   M U

Cloze activities are now frequently used in classrooms. A variation which always appeals to the children involves group or teamwork to provide the missing words.

Divide the children into groups of five or six and elect a captain for each team. Give all the children a copy of the cloze activity, which they read. They then work in their groups and must arrive at a consensus as to which is the best word to place in the blanks, given the context of the reading material. The captain records the group decision, and is the arbiter if there is a deadlock.

At the end, all groups come together. Read the passage and ask the groups to take it in turns to supply the missing words. Encourage discussion if the groups disagree about the suitability of a word. Stimulate originality of thought; discuss whether or not a particular word is appropriate, given the context, and suggest variations and improvements.

---

30   Cacophony: What's the Title?
LISTENING   M U
PURE LUCK

The teacher thinks of a title of a book, a song, or a film, e.g. *Finn Family Moomintroll*. She then selects three children who are each secretly given a word —
   Child 1 — Finn
         2 — Family
         3 — Moomintroll

At a given signal each child must say his or her word **at exactly the same time**.

The group repeats the title over and over, as children call out their guesses. Usually one word is guessed correctly after 2 or 3 repeats. The child who finally guesses the complete title thinks of a new one, and selects a team which contains the same number as the title, e.g. *The Wind in the Willows* will require 5 people.

They then leave the room to be given their words, and to have a whispered rehearsal.

This is remarkably popular with older children.

It *can* be done with Grades 1 and 2, using Nursery Rhyme titles, but they need a lot of help and practice — and you have to be with them — outside the room — while the rest of the class is teacherless (and probably rioting).

So we advise that unless you are strong and experienced, or extremely courageous — don't try this with little children.

2 It's Moments Like These You Need...

When it has been raining for 36 hours non-stop and you are in the errant 4/5 composite again ...! When your very last idea ran out at 3.22 on a Thursday afternoon; when the outsize buffoon from 6D deliberately defies you .... During moments like these you need something to soothe, to quieten, or to entertain for those five or so L O N G minutes until the bell goes.

The ideas presented here may not all be educationally profound: some of them are designed merely to entertain, but you'll be surprised. They all involve movement, talking, listening, interaction. Try them!

1 It's Moments Like These You Need Minties!
MANUAL DEXTERITY   M U

Since we've used their ad as our chapter heading, it's only fair to repay the favour. Always keep a packet of Minties in your Bag of Tricks — your reputation with the children will be greatly enhanced: What was that old saying "The way to a child's heart is through his stomach"?

Give each child a minty and see who can tear the wrapper up into the longest strip of paper.

The winner may be given two minties and — if you're particularly rich or generous — the rest of the class could be given one minty as a consolation prize.

2 Unclenching Fists
ORAL LANGUAGE   J M U

One partner clenches his fist; the other is given thirty seconds to think of a way to get his partner to unclench it. Make a few rules about whining and wounding, bloodshed and bones. When the time is up, ask those who were successful to tell how they succeeded.

We have been absolutely amazed, when trying this activity with our classes. Nearly every child uses brute force and tries to prize his partner's fingers apart. On one occasion there was only one successful unclenching team — modestly we add that it was us! Virginia said to Peter, "Peter, my dear friend, would you please unclench your fist?" "Certainly," he replied, and promptly did so. Bribery sometimes works, and vile threats occasionally succeed. Discuss with the children acceptable alternatives.

Since writing our first draft, there have been a few different methods tried by children. Several children in Grade 2 tickled their partners unmercifully, thus succeeding in unclenching the fists without force. Another tried fortune telling. "Would you like me to tell your fortune? If so, I need to see the palm of your left hand." This was the clenched fist so the clencher declined the offer!

3 Because
ORAL LANGUAGE   M U

Use the list of 31 *Because* statements on page 126 (Sheet 9).

A child chooses a number between 1 and 31. Read the statement, and the child must repeat it, adding his own reason (which can be funny or sensible).

A few examples:

Roses are red because . . . (they are not black).

Teachers teach because . . . (they love inflicting pain on students).

We come to school because . . . (we are masochists).

Once everyone ate butter. Margarine rose to fame because . . . (of the Clancy Brothers' chanting song *A-hem* which ends with the line: It's because you've got the whooping cough and eat margarine!)

*The Olympic Games may as well be
cancelled from now on because . . . .* (Robert
de Castella didn't win the marathon).

---

4 Who's That Talking Behind My Back?
LISTENING   J M U

A child is out the front, facing the board, with
his back to the class. Someone in the class
says "Who am I?" The child has to identify the
speaker by his or her voice. They may disguise
their voices to make it more difficult. The child
who identifies the voice then goes out the
front for her turn.

---

5 Foreverandeverandeverandeverandeve
STORYTELLING   J M U
DEVELOPING PATIENCE

You could introduce this activity by telling the
children in a dramatic way that they are going
to hear a long and interesting story which
needs much careful concentration.

Neverending stories

Pete and Repeat were sitting in a tree.
Pete fell off — who was left? Repeat.
Pete and Repeat were sitting in a tree.
Pete fell off — who was left? Repeat.
Pete and Repeat . . . .

It was a dark and stormy night and all the
sailors were sitting in the cabin. "Tell us
a story," said the First Mate to the
Captain, and so he began, 'It was a dark
and stormy night and all the sailors were
sitting in the cabin. "Tell us a story," said
the First Mate to the Captain, and so he
began . . . .

There is an old folk tale from Burma,
which begins —
One elephant gets in the way of lots of
people
Two elephants get in the way of lots
more
Three elephants get in the way of lots of
people
Four elephants get in the way of lots of
more . .
. . Fifty-six elephants get in the way of
lots of people . .
. . One hundred and four elephants . . .
. . Two hundred and thirty elephants . . .

That is all there is to the "story", but it is
alarming (for the over-burdened storyteller)
that children take so long to catch on. We have
been known to reach astronomical numbers of
elephants before they groan for us to stop.
Many wait patiently for something to happen,
probably thinking "This story has a very slow
build up — it must have a terrific climax!"

---

6 Ventriloquists' Quests
ORAL LANGUAGE   M U

Choose children to say a sentence without
moving their lips. Have heats, semi-finals and
finals. You can use normal sentences in the
heats, but make sure that the finals are very
difficult. Use many words which require clear
diction, and crisp delivery, e.g. Bill brought a
brand new umbrella from his mother's
brother's farm.

Perhaps this could be extended to the use of
puppets in a play for a junior class.

7 Twelves
MATHS   M U
SOCIAL INTERACTION

Children work with partners, hands behind
their backs. When the teacher calls "NOW!"
children hold out their hands, showing any
number of fingers from none to twelve. The
winners are those whose combined fingers
add up to twelve.

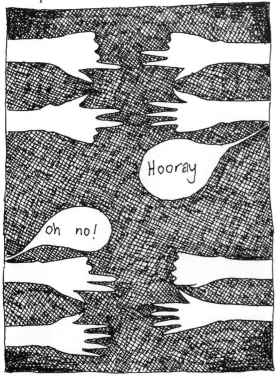

8 Tennis Elbow Foot
ORAL LANGUAGE   M U

Establish the rules of tennis and how to score.
Use a time device, or the regular beat of two
wooden blocks. Server says a word, e.g.*leaf*.
Receiver, during the time given, must supply a
word that links with leaf, e.g. *branch*, and the
game continues: *tree, bough, twig, trunk,
wood, fire, heat, summer* . . . . .

9 Shhhhhh!
LISTENING   J M U

Secret sounds — a very simple activity, but
always liked. The children close their eyes and
attempt to identify the exact sound, produced
by the teacher or classmate, of objects found
around the room. (Scratching the chalkboard
with fingernails, scribbling on a sheet of paper,
clicking two shells together, lighting a match,
scrumpling up a page from a book — rip it out
first.)

    Other children might attempt to recreate the
sound, and the class will estimate how well
they have done it.

10 Tongue Twisting Competition
ORAL LANGUAGE   M U

Similar in organisation to the *Ventriloquists'
Quests*, described above. Have heats and finals.
Get each child (or as many as you can fit in
the time available) to say tricky tongue twisters
as quickly as they can.
    Tim took three thumb tacks.
    Seven shining soldiers.
    Theophilous Thistle, the successful
    thistle-sifter.
    Shun summer sunshine!
    Seven silly sheep shilly-shallied south.
    Sixty sick soldiers sight a sinking ship.
    Caesar sighed and seized the scissors.

Have a presentation, and make a tongue
twister badge for the winner of the Grand
Final.
    (This would, of course, take more than 5
minutes, but you can use odd minutes here
and there by quickly giving each child in the
class a chance to try one of the twisters.
Usually, they dissolve into giggles after the
second attempt — which means you could
just manage the whole class in that time.)

11 Standing Ovations
SELF ESTEEM   J M U

We love this idea and the book in which we found it: *PLAYFAIR, Everybody's Guide to Non-Competitive Play* by Matt Weinstein and Joel Goodman (Impact Publishers, California, 1980). The authors write —

> Why should performing artists be the only ones who get to savor a standing ovation? We all deserve it! A standing ovation should be reserved not only for a special occasion, but for a special person as well. And that means all of us! It feels wonderful to receive, and it can be incredibly energising to give one, too . . .
>
> Of course it happens on occasion that the leader paints such an attractive portrait of group support that everyone rushes up to receive some, leaving no-one in the audience to give the standing ovation . . .
>
> At a university in Ohio, so many people responded to an invitation to come up on to the stage to receive some group support that the entire stage sank slowly to the ground under their combined weight.

In a classroom, you could ask if anyone is feeling a bit depressed or sad. Then ask them if they would like a magnificent, thunderous standing ovation. Encourage them to come out the front, and then let fly!

If at any time during the day (or even the year) someone needs a warm fuzzy, let them leap on their desks and shout, "I need a standing ovation!"

We are not altogether convinced about the any time-any place standing ovation. We have the feeling that they might go on all the time! Perhaps just now and then.

Danger
When children begin cheering it very often reaches almost epidemic proportions. Within an instant, the noise increases in volume and time, and even an experienced teacher finds such an occasion difficult to quell.

Practise with a small group, to test the idea — e.g. at a children's party.

12 Icker-Backer
SELECTION METHOD   J M U

This is an old-fashioned counting-out rhyme. When you can't decide which child to choose for a special task, use *Icker-Backer*. Point to each child as you say each word:
Icker-backer soda cracker
Icker-backer boo!
Icker-backer soda cracker
Out goes Y (why) O (oh) U (you).

The person to whom you are pointing when you reach U (you), the last word, is chosen.

Variation
A simple elimination game, which children in all our grades enjoy. Go through the rhyme until every member of the class (except one) has been eliminated. In this case, the last remaining child is the winner. The intense excitement engendered by this insignificant rhyme remains a mystery to us!

There are many more examples of modern children's counting-out rhymes in *Far Out, Brussel Sprout*, edited by June Factor, illustrated by Peter Viska (Oxford University Press).

. . . WET DAY WINNERS

Children often become quite unbalanced on wet days, and if it's windy as well . . . !!
Therefore a balance is needed between activities which the children can do quietly by themselves (e.g. drawings, cut-outs, craft-making — match-stick models or

paddle-pop sticks, cartoons) and activities for small groups. If you have access to any sorts of games, it is a great advantage. There are usually any number of different games in the junior department, but things are often sparse in the senior school. Try Chess, Monopoly, Snakes and Ladders, Ludo, Boggle, Scrabble, Little Professor, Battleships, Noughts and Crosses, Trivial Pursuit.

The children will probably be playing these games at playtime and lunchtime — aim for pleasure and entertainment, not all workworkwork.

Be sure to have a quiet reading time during the day.

As the children are trapped indoors, it is essential that they do some *active* things. Many of the *Sure-Fire Successes* are suitable here e.g. *Statues, Haystacks, Lion Hunt, Switch Around, The Quickest Clown.*

If the rain *does* stop, SEIZE THE OPPORTUNITY — O U T S I D E! Do anything! "Run to the fence, now hop to the gate, now jump with both feet together to that tree!"

Play *Shipwreck* (see page 16) on the netball court.

Or try:

---

1   Hug Tag
SOCIAL INTERACTION   J M U
COUNTING

All the children find a space by themselves on the marked court. The teacher calls a number: "SIX!" The children must rush and form themselves into groups of six. When they have the right number they shoot their arms into the air, and the first group to do so is the winner.

Call out different numbers. Just for fun, occasionally call out "ONES!" Then stop the game.

When you bring them back inside, try a *Quietener* (see the next section, starting on

page 30), then do something settled and formal, such as:

---

2   Dictation
LANGUAGE   M U

Yes, good old-fashioned dictation. Choose a passage of medium difficulty — you don't want it to be too easy or some of them will start playing up. If they are completely scatty, make the dictation piece last until they start moaning that their hands are dropping off. Then say, "Well, that's your fault. When you are sensible again we'll stop dictation and try something you'll really enjoy.." (Perhaps let them choose.) Or try a *Sure Fire Success.*

---

3   Describing a Mordillo Poster
ART   M U
WRITTEN LANGUAGE

It would be a good idea to keep a few Mordillo posters in your bag of tricks. Children love them, and they often notice things that adults don't.

Here is a Grade 6 interpretation of a Mordillo poster in which a huge bed is balanced precariously on top of a hill:

> While he was sleeping, a mound grew right under his bed. He woke up and realised he was having his dream lady for the night — tonight. So he brought some steps and a rope. He then put his ladder up the mound and the rope up at the very top. Then after picking up his dream lady he is bringing her up his steps to the bed.

If you don't have a Mordillo poster, use some other picture, or borrow one from the library — an interesting chart. You could also ask the children to describe the classroom.

This activity is really only a slight variation of the old picture chat, but we have found that children enjoy this method of written description, while we both remember picture chats with some distaste.

4 Noughts and Crosses
MATHS   M U
LANGUAGE

Nine chairs are arranged at the front of the room in the form of a noughts and crosses shape. Large cards are prepared with Os and Xs.

The basis for having a turn may be spelling words correctly, saying tables, getting number facts right, general knowledge quiz, etc. Children who qualify then collect an O or X card and sit in the chair of their choice. The game then proceeds in the normal fashion. It might be an idea to divide the class into 2 teams — the Os and the Xs. The teacher or leader asks a question, and the first person to call out the answer wins the card.

Of course *Noughts and Crosses* is an excellent wet day activity for groups of two at their tables, desk or on the floor. A variation which they will enjoy is playing noughts and crosses to lose — the winner loses, and the loser wins — i.e. if you get three Os or Xs in a row, your opponent wins.

Another variation is to play with a 16 square grid (i.e. six lines instead of four).

5 Tear A Turtle
ART   J M U

Buy a newspaper on your way to work.

Ask the class to tear out the shape of any animal you name — a turtle, a tomcat, a tiger, lion, mouse, cow . . . They are not allowed to draw the shape first — it must be torn. When completed, display all the efforts and award a prize (a clean sheet of newspaper!). Entries could be numbered, and the class could make judging score sheets. Thus, after everyone has torn a turtle, everyone can have a turn at judging.

6 Decapitated Headlines
LANGUAGE   M U
MEDIA

This might be another thing to include in your bag of tricks — or the class could help you to make a set. Cut an article from a newspaper — preferably one which has a catchy title. Cut the title or headline off and stick it onto thin red card, then stick the main story on a different coloured card. You would need at least twenty or thirty. We have built our sets up over the years, adding funnier ones, and taking out the more serious.

You can use these cards in several ways. The two most common are:

i A simple matching exercise. Find the right headline to go with a particular paragraph.
ii Choose a headline and create your own story to match it. Or do the reverse: choose a paragraph or story, and invent a catchy headline.

7 Where are Fred, Snoopy and Snake?
LANGUAGE   M U
SEQUENCING

(They're cartoon characters — just in case you don't know them.)

Save up the cartoons for a week or so. Cut them up and stick them onto coloured card.

Then cut the cartoons into strips. Place all the pieces in a cardboard box — or perhaps a plastic lunchbox might be better — and ask the children to sort them out.

Some teachers leave the cartoon strips intact, but use correction fluid to delete all the words. Children are then asked to tell the story of the cartoon.

Variations

After examining and discussing some cartoons, let the children make up their own. Give them a few topics, such as

Late for School
An Embarrassing moment for the teacher
Caught!
Too Late
Baby in the Honey Jar

or let them provide their own subjects and labels.

Talk about the comic strips with the children. Explore how a story is developed, then children may tell their own stories, or re-tell famous episodes from stories in comic strip form.

---

8   Creative Colouring In
ART   J M U
DESIGN

There are many booklets of these available from toyshops and artshops. *Altair* is one. The designs are extremely intricate and take ages and ages to complete, thus making them a perfect wet-day winner. Use Sheets 35 and 39 as starters.

There are also many *Anti-Colouring-In* books, where children are given some shapes and lines and are asked to complete the picture.

Using *Mathomats* (an invaluable mathematical aid) children will be able to make up their own patterns and designs to colour in.

---

9   Sale of the Century
ANY SUBJECT   M U

The game is played in similar fashion to the T.V. game. Play three rounds with four children in each; winners of each round and highest scoring loser go into the final. Each child starts with twenty points; five points are awarded for a correct answer, five points are taken off for an incorrect answer, or for no response. The first hand up answers the question. Each contestant has a scorer to keep a running total on the chalkboard.

---

10   Land Hockey
PHYSICAL EDUCATION   M U

This game can be played inside, but preferably in a multi-purpose room or gym. The size of the teams can vary from five to ten. For a full class, play a knockout competition.

You need two benches or long stools as goals. Lay these on their sides at each end of the hall. Colour bands are useful to distinguish the teams. A medium sized rubber or plastic ball is best; the ideal is a volley ball.

The teacher rolls the ball into play to start the game. The ball is hit with the flat hand towards the goal. There is no out of bounds as balls ricocheting off the walls are still in play. The ball cannot be picked up or kicked. Any transgression of the rules results in a free throw for the opposing side. A goal is scored when the ball hits the front face of the bench. Any child may score. There is no one attacker or goalie, but all children must be ready to attack or defend as the occasion warrants it.

11 The Most Common Letter
LANGUAGE   M U

This is an excellent wet day winner because it is an activity which the child can do alone; it demands concentration, and all that is necessary is a pencil, some paper, and a book or cutting from a newspaper.

Tell the children that they are going to discover which is the most used letter in the English language. Ask them to make a guess of their own.

Ask them to count out the first 200 letters of any story. Make a soft pencil mark on the 200th letter. Write the letters of the alphabet down a sheet, then start at the first letter and tally the number of times each letter occurs.

a   *////*
b
c   *//*
d   */*
e   *//// //*
f   */*

The total for each letter can be tallied on the chalkboard. Discover whether one letter consistently tallies higher than the other letters, and work out the totals.

12 Complete the Picture
ART   J M U
SYMMETRY

Provide the children with old magazines and newspapers. Ask them to find a picture of a face which they would like to copy. They then tear that page from the magazine and cut the face in half. Throw the other half away. Paste the half-face onto a piece of paper or card. Then try to draw the other side of the face.

The completed pictures make an excellent display.

Variation

An excellent variation is when the class is divided into two teams. Team A stands at one side of the hall, each member being about one metre away from the next. Team B stands at the other side of the hall, spaced in the same way as Team A. One child from each team is in the middle.

The teacher throws a ball into the middle and the opposing players have to bat the ball with their hands through the lines of the other team to score a goal. The children at the sides have to defend by batting the ball with their hands back towards the centre.

13　Hangman
LANGUAGE　　M U

A game which is best played by two people. One player chooses a word and writes down the first and the last letters, using dashes (or dots) for all the letters in between.

The other person has to try to guess the word. She suggests letters one at a time. If she chooses a letter not in the word, her partner draws in a part of the gallows, and with each wrong answer a part of the body of the hanged man is added.

Ten wrong guesses mean death by the gallows!

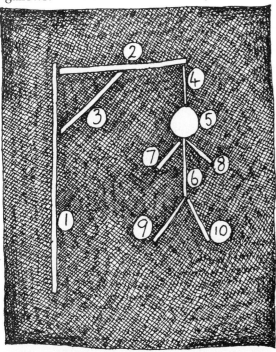

... QUIETENERS

After a vigorous activity, an exciting sporting match, or whenever you feel the need, try one of the following activities. This will give you a rest, and the children a chance to settle down, so that your next lesson will proceed smoothly.

1　Hold Your Breath Competition
U

Absolutely guaranteed to quieten! Time the children and see who can hold his or her breath for the the longest time.

Try to ensure that no one dies because of over-enthusiasm. Warn them: You can't win if you expire!

2　Stop for 1 minute 35 seconds
LISTENING　　M U

Stop for 1 minute 35 seconds, then write down everything — every single thing — that you heard.

The class will be perfectly quiet as the children listen intently, and after the time is up, they write down everything as quickly as they can. Discussion will follow.

3　Hiss the Word TEST at the Class
?#$%**!!　　M U

Few words have such power to create panic as the fatal four letter word: TEST! Anguished moans of *What for?*, *What sort of test?*, *Why?* can be predicted.

Perhaps you could announce solemnly that Someone in the Education Department (i.e. V.F and P.D.) has asked you to conduct tests in several schools, to see if classes are working up to scratch.

Say: "Please put your name on the top of the sheet in front of you, and work very hard, without a sound. I will let you know in due course if your results are better than those of other schools." In this case, it may be wise to devise a formal test in spelling, or maths, or handwriting. Or, you could try one of our *Sheets* from Chapter 4.

4   Shut-eye
DISCIPLINE STRATEGY   J M U

Someone told us that if children are noisy, you call out loudly, "SHUT YOUR EYES!"

Apparently there is some connection between sight and speech, because when children's eyes are shut, their mouths shut down, too.

We have vague reservations about the success of this one, but it's worth a try — and it has worked for us with many classes (but not all)!

5   Bossy Roll Call
DISCIPLINE STRATEGY   J M U

When we were at teachers' college (bring out the violins!) there was a subject called Teaching Method. One of our lecturers assured us that we would have perfect control throughout the whole year if we started off on the right foot. His suggestion was that as soon as the children entered the room on the very first day, we would take out the roll. The idea was to read the child's name very sternly, make him or her stand during this time, and then fix a solemn stare at him for about six

seconds. The child then sat down, and you moved on to the next name.

One teacher at Rosevern, being an obedient young teacher, began to follow these instructions. By the time she had reached the C's, the whole class was in utter chaos. Children were clutching their sides in agonies of laughter. She only did it once, but all through the year, whenever she asked them what they'd like to do (these were the days before Five Minute Fillers) they would plead in rapture, "Please read the roll like you did on the first day".

6   Write Six 6-letter Words
VOCABULARY DEVELOPMENT   M U

Set a time limit, allow children to use dictionaries, and see who can finish first.

Write six 6-letter words.
Write seven 7-letter words.
Write eight 8-letter words.
Write nine 9-letter words.
Write ten 10-letter words.
Write eleven 11-letter words.

This keeps them feverishly busy!

Perhaps, at the conclusion, children could swap interesting words they have discovered. They could make a list of their twenty most fascinating newly discovered words, and try to learn how to use and to spell them in the weeks to come.

7   Body Language: Talking Without Words
SOCIAL INTERACTION   J M U
SENSORY DEVELOPMENT

Children write down a short simple message on a scrap of paper, but don't show it to their partner. They then try to communicate, without speaking, what the message is. The partner writes down on a piece of paper each word that he thinks is being communicated. The communicator confirms or denies whether the word is correct by a nod or shake of the head.

Before beginning, you could talk to the children about non-verbal communication and suggest the kind of messages which would be easiest to begin with — e.g.

I — pointing to self
like — hug, puckered lips
you — pointing to partner

---

8 Pneumonoultramicroscopicsilicovolcano -coniosis
SHOWING OFF   U

Introduce with great drama and relish a very long word. Write it on the board in ENORMOUS letters. Then say, "Right, here's a little spelling test. I will allow you six minutes to learn this word, then I'm going to test you."

The dramatic impact is increased a hundred-fold if you can memorise the word yourself; in fact there would be little point in trying this activity unless you could master it — and it's easy:
Do what we always tell the younger children — break the word up into little words:
Pneumono — ultra — microscopic — silico — volcano — coniosis.
Easy, isn't it?
(It means a disease that miners working underground contract from breathing in tiny particles of silicon dust.)

---

9 U.S.S.R.
READING   J M U
LITERATURE

In our day this activity was called *Free*

Readin', and it simply meant that we all chose something to read — and read it without noise for a certain amount of time. Now there are whole books devoted to this topic. Theses have been written, and many a chapter in many a book!

U.S.S.R. means Uninterrupted Sustained Silent Reading; other programs call it D.E.A.R. — Drop Everything and Read. The only difference which we can see between this and Free Readin' is that — ideally — every person in the whole school from the School Principal to the ladies in the canteen downs tools and picks up a book and reads it at the same time each day.

If you are a visitor to the school you could ask the children if they usually have reading time: when is it, or when would they like to read? Select a time, and if there is very little reading material in the room, go to the librarian and beg her for all the picture books in the T section. (This saves problems in sorting them out when returning them. If she's a good sport, she'll count the number of books, and trust you to return them straight after reading time.)

In our classrooms, we begin every day with Quiet Reading. Between the hours of 9.00 and 9.30, not a word is spoken, only the frenzied sounds of pages being turned. One of our dearest memories is when Sam, a macho 11-year-old non-reader, called out (at the top of his voice) "THAT WAS A BLOODY ACE BOOK!!" when he finished *The Day the Spaceship Landed* by Beman Lord (Nelson).

---

10 U.S.S.W.
WRITING   M U

We just made that title up on the spot. It means Uninterrupted Sustained Silent Writing. Teacher and children all write together on a topic (or topics) chosen by the teacher or the children; or perhaps they may prefer the more private *Speed Writing* described in Chapter 1 (see page 6).

---

11   Guess a Minute
ESTIMATION   M U

All that is required is a teacher with a stop watch. Children volunteer one by one, or group by group, to guess when a minute is up. If the group method is used, you will need a sharp-eyed scrutineer. The unfailing popularity of this game is just as much a mystery to us as it may be to you.

---

12   Read in a Quiet Voice
LITERARY APPRECIATION   J M U

Select a popular or very interesting poem or story. Begin to read in a normal voice but become quiet and even more quiet. The children will strain to listen as your voice reaches whisper level.

... NUISANCE NEUTRALISERS

Picture the scene. It is 8.57. The phone rings and at the other end the Principal is sounding even more desperate than usual: "Can you come? It doesn't matter when you arrive. We'll be eternally grateful ..."

You arrive. The Principal greets you, dripping with gratitude. He'll lead you to your class. But there's no need to lead you. You know it will be *that* grade six, and you heard them from outside the school as you drove up in the car.

The scene is not an uncommon one. It is the lot of the relieving teacher to land the rampant grade 6 or the renegade 4. You are not surprised, but instead, perplexed. The question, really, is a simple one: how are you going to survive the next seven hours?

Of course, if you possibly can, apply the tried and true procedures which are successful with nearly all grades:

- Establish a firm, friendly tone from the moment you meet the children. The first ten minutes are crucial. Clearly define rules and codes of behaviour. Let the children know exactly what is expected of them..
- Take immediate and mild disciplinary action to halt misbehaviour or inattention, rather than over-reacting.
- Move the trouble makers away from the troublesome areas. Closer to you (with their backs to the class) is better. But don't create a combatant situation. Use subtle means of removing them from the place of trouble.
- Catch children being good. Use this as a means of discipline. Good behaviour is rewarded by privileges. Quite often this has a ripple effect.
- Beware of pleas like "... but we don't do it that way ...", or "Miss C always lets us out." Tell them that they are your responsibility for the day. But at the same time *don't* ignore class rules. If the whole grade has previously negotiated a set of rules, ask to see them. (They are usually printed and displayed somewhere in the classroom.) Discuss the rules with the chidren. This can be an excellent method of maintaining discipline in the room.
- Use the tried and true commands to maintain order. "STOP!" or "Freeze!" or "Fold arms" means that the children immediately cease what they are doing, and listen.

  Insist on "Two straight lines" when the class is moving en masse from one place to another.

  A short sharp burst on the whistle during Phys. Ed. means that all children immediately stop what they are doing and return to the teacher.
- Learn the children's names as quickly as

possible. Discipline is severely inhibited if the wrong child (or no child in particular) is castigated for a certain wrong doing.

- Tell the children that their written work will be corrected, and make sure that this is done.
- Prepare well. Many discipline problems arise because classroom instruction and management is poor, causing children to lose interest and thus become troublemakers. As a general rule the grade which is kept working industriously (but not simply with busy work) is easier to handle. After you get to know them better, it is possible to relax more and try less structured, more open ended activities.

The tried and true procedures work most of the time for most grades but some children on some days just run wild. And if you only have the class for a short time it is impossible to learn all their quirks and wiles, or to adopt some of the classical behaviour modification programs.

The suggestions presented here have worked for us. The problem with many of them is that they work too well. We have been asked more than once by our most difficult grades if they can have a repeat dose of some of our "neutralisers". *Calligraphy* is perennially popular, and children often ask again for *Dead Sheep*, but very few — we must admit — have ever made a second request for *Copy Out the Dictionary* or the *3.15 Long Tot!*

1   Copy Out the Dictionary

This is the most feared punishment of all. Worse than The Strap, worse than Picking Up Papers, worse than Standing Outside the Office. Give the sinner two chances, then point to a place *away* from his classmates, e.g. under the chalkboard, with his back to the class. Use a chair as a desk, and a cushion as his seat.

Hand him a dictionary, a huge wad of paper and command, "Copy out THE ENTIRE dictionary starting from A!"

On one occasion, Ross (you all know Ross!) misbehaved so often that the next day when we were investigating another misdeed, he ran across and fell to his knees, imploring, "Not the dictionary! Please! Please! Anything ANYTHING but the dictionary! Me poor hand'll never be the same again!"

2   Calligraphy

We used to call this *transcription*, and it really was a boring activity. Calligraphy is a form of handwriting most children seem to enjoy, perhaps because they can concentrate on doing their very best work without having to think too hard. And it has the Pan-like quality of calming the noisiest children.

Using their most beautiful handwriting, and most artistic headings and borders, children must copy a poem which the teacher has written on the board. This must be done in utter silence.

Instead of writing a poem on the board, if you have made a collection of poetry cards, all you have to do is to hand each child a card.

3   Lines
Lines
Lines
Lines

This old-fashioned, oft-delivered method of punishment was given so often in our day that it ceased to become a punishment. It was just a normal part of school life. With modern educational methods, it has been banished or forgotten by kindlier, more recent teachers. We are proud to announce it as a Born Again Punishment.

Never mind about "I must not talk in

school" or "I must not be late". Make far more regal pronouncements:
"I must pay for my loquacity by fulfilling this onerous assignation as an extra-curricular activity."

We say to our classes, when they have tried us to the limits, "Right! STOP! From NOW ON (*in ominous voice*) the first person who so much as moves a muscle will be given ONE HUNDRED LINES!! The second person who transgresses will be given THREE HUNDRED LINES!!!" (Sigh! Moan! Gasp!) — and then, with great drama — "and if there should be a third person, she or he will do ONE THOUSAND LINES!!"

We have never had to administer this last threat, and have only rarely given the 300. 100 lines usually suffice and subdue. At Rosevern the Great Bubble Gum Blight of 1984 was cured in this way.

4 Hands on Heads

Used occasionally, this old method still works. "Hands on heads" is shorthand speech which children correctly interpret (through years of repetition and reinforcement) as "Sit still, be quiet and listen to the teacher — or else!"

5 3.31

If it's close to morning recess, write 10.30 on the board in LARGE letters. If you have asked for attention and some children are still not obeying, brandish your hand across the board, swipe at the 30 and change it to 10.31. If another misdemeanor occurs, change it to 10.32 . . . 10.33 . . . 10.34. They will very quickly get the message that unless they are quiet they will miss out on a lot of recess.

At lunch time, try the same thing, or near home time a large 3.30 works wonders!

Variation

Times Two

Say: Right — you're wasting *our* time. I'll waste yours. For every minute you keep us waiting, I'll multiply it by two, and keep you waiting at lunch, sport, or home time.

Check the school's policy on keeping in for these two neutralisers.

6 Punishment Pack, or Forty Forfeits

Make a pack of cards and write a punishment on each one. (In Victorian days this was a Parlour Game called forfeits, which usually read: Kiss the lady with the blue ribbon . . .) Ours will be less Victorian!

Just before the recess bell goes, ask the offender to take a card from the pack, and to do what is requested thereon.

Pick up fifty papers from the yard.

Make up 40 automatic response equations for the class to do tomorrow.

Hop around the classroom once, calling "Naughty, naughtier, naughtiest".

Say: "My behaviour should be less ostentatious" twenty times.

7 Dead Sheep

Usually played with younger children, but perhaps you could try *Dead Elephants* with older classes.

Just cry out "DEAD SHEEP!" and immediately every child in the class must fall to the floor and become dead sheep.

All movement — except quiet breathing — is banned.

8 The 72 Times Table

At any time of the day when trouble looms, point at a trouble maker, and say in a steely tone: "Ben! Stop what you're doing RIGHT NOW, and write down the 72 times table".

If the children settle down, allow them to continue their normal classroom activities, but at the first sign of misbehaviour, repeat: "Write out the 97 times table, . . . the 876 times table" and so on.

(Thanks to Robert Csoti for this one.)

9 3.15 Long Tot — the Punishment to end all Punishments

In the olden days (long before either of us was/were in our nappy/nappies), long suffering students picked up their steel nibbed pens, dipped them in the inkwells and began to scratch their way through the Friday Afternoon Long Tot. Not until it was completed and perfectly correct, both horizontally and vertically could they go home. Below is a true example of what our forebears bore:

THE FEDERAL ARITHMETIC

EXERCISE 48 — LONG TOTS

Add vertically and across the page:-

£	s.	d.		£	s.	d.		£	s.	d.
(1) 4786	17	$8\frac{1}{2}$	(2)	784	19	$6\frac{1}{2}$	(3)	3587	16	$5\frac{1}{2}$
758	6	9		89	17	$5\frac{1}{4}$		952	7	$9\frac{1}{4}$
9756	16	$8\frac{3}{4}$		698	14	9		6849	15	7
5687	15	$7\frac{1}{2}$		239	15	$6\frac{3}{4}$		395	14	6
8578	19	$6\frac{3}{4}$		578	13	9		857	9	$5\frac{1}{2}$
879	18	$9\frac{1}{2}$		3587	16	$5\frac{1}{2}$		549	16	$3\frac{1}{4}$
785	13	$8\frac{1}{4}$		952	7	$9\frac{1}{4}$		98	15	$6\frac{3}{4}$
2543	15	$6\frac{1}{2}$		6849	15	7		3987	19	10
958	19	$11\frac{1}{4}$		395	14	6		756	8	$7\frac{3}{4}$
7854	14	$10\frac{1}{2}$		857	9	$5\frac{1}{2}$		849	7	9
784	19	$6\frac{1}{2}$		549	16	$3\frac{1}{4}$		586	14	$11\frac{1}{2}$
89	17	$5\frac{1}{4}$		98	15	$6\frac{3}{4}$		345	16	$9\frac{1}{4}$
698	14	9		3987	19	10		954	8	$7\frac{1}{2}$
239	15	$6\frac{3}{4}$		756	8	$7\frac{3}{4}$		2763	15	8
578	13	9		849	7	9		678	13	$11\frac{3}{4}$
3587	16	$5\frac{1}{2}$		586	14	$11\frac{1}{2}$		958	17	5
952	7	$9\frac{1}{4}$		345	16	$9\frac{1}{4}$		3795	14	$6\frac{1}{2}$
6849	15	7		954	8	$7\frac{1}{2}$		798	19	$11\frac{3}{4}$
395	14	6		2763	15	8		86	13	$9\frac{1}{2}$
857	9	$5\frac{1}{2}$		678	13	$11\frac{3}{4}$		637	15	$8\frac{1}{4}$

Only your most ingenious miscreants could complete this pre-decimalised Long Tot, but a modern version, given at the appropriate moment (12.05, 3.15) may have a similar effect.

3 A Day in the Grades

Here are some ideas to try if you find that you have to take the Grade for a day.

We have given examples for each grade level, and two for Grade 6. Remember, they are just examples. We hope you will use them as springboards, rather than prescriptive rules to be followed slavishly.

We have based the ideas on themes, and for some we've deliberately chosen way-out themes (e.g. *Long Nose Day*) just to show what you can do with even the most unlikely topic.

One way to ensure success is to be prepared. (Ask the Boy Scouts!) Some golden rules which have always worked for us are:

1 Prepare some material (poems, chants, maths, songs) on charts, chalkboard or fabric before the day begins.

2 Don't forget your bag of tricks (see page 185). If all else fails, grab your favourite trick/poem/book/idea. Stay cool and L A U N C H off!!!

3 Prepare a set of worksheets which are of general interest, and which will keep the class busy, amused and quiet for at least twenty minutes while you catch your breath.
(Probably you won't use these, but it is comforting to know that they are there.)

At the beginning of each separate *Day in the Grades* we have listed a number of preparation jobs, and materials to gather, prior to 9 a.m. This may seem to be an onerous task but we promise you that it is worth it. We suggest that, where possible, you put a lot of this material (poems, diagrams, songs, puzzles) onto charts or wall hangings. The latter are extremely successful, because if you use a waterproof marker on material, all you need to do is to press and starch after each use and your charts will always look as good as new.

Theme: Animals

PREPARATION
1 Make copies of Sheet 13, *3 Frogs and 3 Snakes*.
2 Try to find the story *The Three Billy Goats Gruff*, or read the summary on pages 40–41.
3 Make copies of Sheet 34, *The Three Billy Goats Gruff*.
4 Newsprint for Cut and Paste activity.
5 Two cane hoops and a quantity of bean bags.
6 Read the summary of the story *That's What Friends are For* (pages 43–45).

9.00–9.10

Bring the children in. Because these children are young, they need to feel secure in the classroom and it could be traumatic to have a new teacher. Explain who you are, why you're there, and that their teacher (name her) will be back as soon as she's better.

There will probably be some day-to-day preliminary duties to be performed, but try to keep these to a minimum so that a friendly and happy atmosphere will prevail.

9.10–9.35

POEM
The theme of the day is centred around animals and this poem by Evelyn Beyer is an ideal beginning.
First of all read the poem without explanation:

Jump or Jiggle

Frogs jump
Caterpillars hump

Worms wiggle
Bugs jiggle

Rabbits hop
Horses clop

Snakes slide
Seagulls glide

Mice creep
Deer leap

Puppies bounce
Kittens pounce

Lions stalk
But —
I walk!

Evelyn Beyer

Before reading it a second time, tell the children that you want
them to listen *very* carefully because you are going to ask some
questions to find out who are the best listeners.
Read the poem again, then ask questions like these:
  Which animal jumps?
  What do worms do?
  What animals go CLOP?
  How do seagulls fly?
  Which animal pounces?
  Which animal bounces?
  Do mice creep or crawl?
  Now this is a very hard one: What does a lion do?
  Have we missed any?
Read the poem again, if the children want to hear the poet's
answers.
  They should be familiar with the animals in the poem by
now, so when you read the poem this time, ask the children to
stand up and make all the different movements as you name
them: E.g. "Frogs jump . . ." (all children jump like frogs)
  Another way (but more difficult to organise) would be to
divide the class into groups of animals — a worm group, a
snake group, and so on — although for the last line they all
stand up straight and walk around the room. (Quietly or
stomping — it depends on you.)
  We've said this before — but for Preps it is most important of
all: make sure that the children understand your STOP signal,
whether it be a bell, two hand claps, a drum beat, the tinkle of a
fork against a glass, or a policemen's hand up STOP signal.

9.35–10.20

MATHS: THREE
The children will be doing Sheet 13, *3 Frogs and 3 Snakes*. But
prior to this much oral discussion about three should occur.
Choose from some of these activities:

 i **First, second, third**
   Are you the first in your family, or second or third?
ii **Auditory activities**
   Recall three numbers: 10, 2, 4 or 6, 8, 5
   or
   Recall three animals: bear, tiger, dog

39

iii Visual discrimination

Display three items e.g. book, comb, pencil. Take one away. Which one did I take away?

iv Triangles

Use attribute blocks, or shapes made of vinyl or card.

Display a large triangle. Talk about its three sides.

Allow the children to sort attribute blocks. Separate the triangular shapes from the others.

There are excellent follow-up activities using shapes which you probably will not have time to complete today but which could occur later. E.g. what things in the environment have a triangular shape? Our children discovered sea–saw, tent, sailboat, house, mountain.

Art might follow a detailed examination of the triangle shape. (Turn it on its side, upside down, flat etc.). Get the children to cut out triangular shapes — have the outlines run off. They then paste their triangles onto a sheet of paper and create scenes around the triangles.

Allow sufficient time before play to talk about the sheets after the children have completed them.

If there is time, children could talk about animals they have seen — as pets, zoo animals, bush animals . . .

10.20	Get ready for recess early. All children wash hands, find play lunch.
	Check to see if you are on duty. Remind the children to go to the toilet in the recess break.
10.30–10.45	Recess
10.45–10.50	Bring children in, count them and then mark the roll. (It's probably a good idea to count them a couple of times during the day.)
10.50–11.15	STORYTIME AND DRAMA: THE THREE BILLY GOATS GRUFF You will probably know the story, and it will certainly be in most libraries, but here is a short summary. The children will help you with the details, we are sure.

The Three Billy Goats Gruff

Once upon a time there were three Billy Goats Gruff. One was called the Little Billy Goat Gruff; the second was called the Middle-sized Billy Goat Gruff and the third was called the Big Billy Goat Gruff. The three goats were very hungry. There was grass on a nearby hill but they were too frightened to go there because under the bridge lurked a wicked troll with eyes as big as saucers and a nose as long as a poker.

The smallest Billy Goat — Little Billy Goat Gruff — decided to take the risk, so away he went — trips-trap-trip-trap over the bridge.

"Who's that trip-trapping over my bridge?" shouted the troll. "It is I, Little Billy Goat Gruff." "Then I'm going to gobble you up!" roared the troll. But Little Billy Goat Gruff persuaded the Troll to wait for his bigger brother. The scene was repeated as Middle-sized Billy Goat Gruff trip-trapped over the bridge. Most of the scene is repeated with the Big Billy Goat Gruff, but this time a battle ensues and Big Billy Goat Gruff hurls the troll into the water. He is never seen again, and the three Billy Goats enjoy the green grass on the other side of the hill.

Choose children to act the story. Props are simple — a chair as the step leading up to the bridge, a table for the bridge, another chair (step), and the children can improvise a green hill.

Retell the story with the children acting the parts.

11.15—12.00

BILLY GOAT ACTIVITIES

Use Sheet 34, which contains pictures of the three Billy Goats, the bridge, the troll, the hill and the river. Children first colour in the pictures. Then they cut out and paste all the illustrations in an appropriate place on a larger sheet of paper (newsprint will do). The troll will probably be under the bridge, but the children will select where the Billy Goats are to be pasted. E.g. the little one may be on the green grassy hill, the middle-sized one may be on the bridge, and the big one may be on the other side of the bridge where there is no grass.

Take the opportunity to reinforce the children's sequencing concepts. Now would be a good time to talk about ordinal numbers. "Show me the first Billy Goat on Jenny's picture." "Where is the third Billy Goat in your picture?" What is the name of the second Billy Goat?"

When most children have finished their sheets, choose some of them to hold up their pictures for discussion. "Anna's Little Billy Goat Gruff is coloured purple!" "Jim's Troll has three eyes." "Sophie's Billy Goat is upside down."

12.00–12.15

Prepare for lunch about 15 minutes before the bell. If there is time to spare, have a little health session on clean hands and good manners (no slurpy chomping like the dreadful Troll!).

12.15–12.30

Supervise lunch

12.30–1.15

Lunch break

1.15–1.30

Count children
SONG: OLD MACDONALD HAD A FARM
Children think up as many animals as they can, and sing the verses in any order. (Teacher points to child whose turn it is, the child names an animal — a pig — and they respond appropriately.)

1.30–1.45

LISTENING GAME: WHICH ANIMAL AM I?
A child is chosen to come out the front and shut her eyes. One child in the audience makes an animal noise ("MOO", "OINK, OINK", "WOOF WOOF", "CHEEP, CHEEP").
The child at the front tries to guess who made the sound, and what animal it was.

1.45

If it is early in the year many Preps get very tired at this time of day. Some grades even have a sleep or rest time. Many other grades at some time during the day have a free choice activity where children are able to play in groups or alone with a variety of educational materials available in most Prep rooms.
We have not allowed such a time in this program — it is up to you to make your own judgement.

1.45–2.10

PHYSICAL EDUCATION GAME: "MOO QUACK! MOO QUACK!"
Talk about the animals and their sounds in *Old MacDonald Had a Farm*.
Then play *Moo Quack! Moo! Quack!*
Beware of chaos.
To play, help the children to form a large circle.

42

Teacher goes from child to child, whispering in each ear either MOO or QUACK.

When the teacher says "GO!" the children close their eyes, hold their hands out in front of them and begin quacking or mooing.

The aim is to get all the ducks in one place, and all the cows in another. Children have to identify by listening very carefully.

The duck team and the cow team could (if there is time) play a short game with bean bags and hoops.
Aim to get as many bean bags in the hoop as possible.

The first child in each team stands on a marked line, facing the hoop.
He throws his bean bag, then sits down on the sidelines, while the second child has a turn. This is repeated until all cows and ducks have had a turn. Add up the bean bags in each hoop. Who won?

2.15–2.30 Recess

2.30–2.50 STORY: THAT'S WHAT FRIENDS ARE FOR
Children find this story most amusing. Here is a summary. Embellish it as much as you wish.

That's What Friends are For

A poor ELEPHANT was lying in the middle of the forest. He had hurt his leg, and that was bad news because today he had planned to visit his cousin at the end of the forest. "Whatever will I do?" he thought. "I know. I'll ask my friends for advice. That's what friends are for!"

43

BIRD flies along: "Why are you lying in the middle of the forest?"

ELEPHANT (explains about his hurt leg, and his cousin.)

BIRD: I know what *I'd* do. I'd just flap my wings and fly to the end of the forest.

ELEPHANT (rueful): Thanks (but he thinks sadly: I don't have any wings).

BIRD: That's O.K. That's what friends are for!

SPIDER: Asks same question as the bird.

ELEPHANT: Replies in the same way as before.

SPIDER: I know what *I'd* do. I'd tuck my sore leg right up, and walk on my seven other legs.

ELEPHANT: Thanks ...

SPIDER: That's O.K. That's what friends are for!

CRAB: As before.

ELEPHANT: Replies as before.

CRAB: I know what *I'd* do. I'd throw off my sore leg and grow another.

ELEPHANT: Thanks.

CRAB: That's O.K. That's what friends are for!

MONKEY: Asks as before.

ELEPHANT: Explains "... and I can't fly, I haven't eight legs, I can't throw off a sore leg and grow another ..."

MONKEY: I know what *I'd* do! I'd swing by my tail from branch to branch.

ELEPHANT: I haven't got a very strong tail, but I DO have a VERY strong trunk. (He reaches his trunk up, up, up to the tree. He lifts himself up ... up ... but he falls — C R A S H ! — poor elephant.)

LION: Same dialogue as before.

I know what *I'd* do. I'd roar so loudly that everyone would come and see what was the matter. I'd roar like this-RROOAARRR!. (Children roar with the lion.)

POSSUM: Comes out of a tree and asks what's wrong.

LION: Explains about the elephant's sore leg, and concludes: we're all giving him advice. After all, that's what friends are for!

POSSUM: No, no, that's not always true. Friends are to **HELP**. Why don't we all go and get the elephant's cousin and bring him right back here to meet his cousin.

So off they went, First the BIRD, then the SPIDER, then the CRAB, the MONKEY, LION and POSSUM. They find the elephant's cousin, bring him back, and they all have a BIG PARTY to celebrate.

ELEPHANT: Thanks, everyone, for helping!
ALL OTHER ANIMALS: That's O.K. That's what friends
are for!

2.50–3.10

ART OR DRAMA
Children may ask to act the story out; others may want to
illustrate a funny part of the story.
Decide what to do.
(If they draw, crayons and bulky newsprint are safest.)

3.10–3.20

POEM

Laughing Time

It was laughing time and the tall Giraffe
Lifted his head and began to laugh:

Ha! Ha! Ha! Ha!

And the Chimpanzee on the ginkgo tree
Swung merrily down with a TEE HEE HEE:

Hee! Hee! Hee! Hee!

"It's certainly not against the law!"
Croaked Justice Crow with a loud guffaw:

Haw! Haw! Haw! Haw!

The dancing Bear who could never say "No"
Waltzed up and down on the tip of his toe:

Ho! Ho! Ho! Ho!

The Donkey daintily took his paw
And around they went: Hee-Haw! Hee-Haw!

Hee-Haw! Hee-Haw!

The Moon had to smile as it started to climb;
All over the world it was laughing time!

Ho! Ho! Ho! Ho! Hee-Haw! Hee-Haw!
Hee! Hee! Hee! Hee! Ha! Ha! Ha! Ha!

William J. Smith

Children could stand up and mime the noises and actions
mentioned in the poem.

45

3.20

Allow time for packing up, putting chairs on tables, school notices in bags, etc.

If there are a few minutes before the bell children could mime any animal and ask other class members to guess what animal they are acting, and what they are doing.

Ask all the children to give you a great big smile as they leave the room at home time.

GRADE 1

Theme: Trees

PREPARATION

1 Draw or find a large picture of a tree.
2 Writing paper for sentences about leaves.
3 Prepare set of labels: *first* to *tenth* (see page 51).
4 Make copies of Sheet 14, *Which Tree Comes First?*
5 Newspaper for *Tearing a Tree.*
6 Large sheets of paper for group work on leaf classification.
7 Large sheets of white paper, scissors, paste, felt pens, coloured pencils and coloured paper for the *Make a Tree* activity.

8.55

Read the advice given on page 37.

9.00–9.10

Settling in

9.15–9.25

GETTING TO KNOW YOU/STORY/DRAMA

From Seed to Tree

Children crouch down and make themselves into a tiny seed shape. Children poke one finger above their heads (ground level). Children begin to stand up . . . and stretch higher . . .

Once upon a time a farmer planted a tiny seed. It was so small you could hardly see it.

It stayed in the ground for a L–O–N–G time. The rain rained, the sun shone and the wind blew until one bright day a very small green shoot popped out of the ground.

A month passed. The rain rained, the sun shone and the wind blew, and the small green shoot grew taller.

Two months passed. The rain rained, the sun shone and the wind blew and the green shoot grew into a plant.

and even higher . . .

Three months passed. The rain rained, the sun shone and the wind blew and the plant changed into a small tree.

    It grew higher . . .

      . . . and higher

      . . . and higher

. . . and higher still . . .
Children stand on
tippy toes, arms
stretching high above
them.

. . . until one proud day it became the tallest tree in the whole forest.

Note: If you want a sad (and quiet) ending add:

Children crash to the
ground, then remain
perfectly still.

And guess what happened: a woodcutter chopped it down until it lay as quiet and still as a stick.

9.25–10.00

TALK — WRITE — READ, AND FOLLOWING DIRECTIONS

Before the children come in draw a large tree on the chalkboard — or find a big colourful picture of a tree.

Talk about trees. Look out the window. How many trees can you see? Do you have a favourite tree? Trees at your house? Fruit trees? What kind?

Fill the chalkboard with sentences about trees. Repeat the words as you write them on the board. Underline words such as *tree, trees, leaf, leaves*. Discuss bark, twig, trunk, branches.

Ask the children to write a sentence on their own sheets of paper, using words from the board. They can then read their sentences to each other or the class. (Keep the paper. Fast finishers may illustrate their sentences later.)

Give children a fresh sheet (or they could use the other side of the first sheet). Tell them they must listen very closely, because they are going to do a drawing with many different things in it. Then give them the instructions. (Allow them plenty of time to complete each stage.)

1 Draw a picture of a big tree with some branches.
2 The tree has a lot of green leaves on it.
3 There is an orange cat in the tree.
4 Dad is underneath the tree. He is looking at the cat.

Allow the children time to discuss their pictures and to show them to the class. Organise a place for them to be displayed.

POEM

Dad and the Cat and the Tree

This morning a cat got
Stuck in our tree.
Dad said, "Right, just
Leave it to me."

The tree was wobbly,
The tree was tall.
Mum said, "For goodness'
Sake don't fall!"

"Fall?" scoffed Dad,
"A climber like me?
Child's play this is!
You wait and see."

He got out the ladder
From the garden shed.
It slipped. He landed
In the flower bed.

"Never mind", said Dad,
Brushing the dirt
Off his hair and his face
And his trousers and shirt,

"We'll try Plan B. Stand
Out of the way!"
Mum said, "Don't fall
Again, O.K.?"

"Fall again?" said Dad.
"Funny joke!"
Then he swung himself up
On a branch. It broke.

Dad landed *wallop*
Back on the deck.
Mum said, "Stop it,
You'll break your neck!"

"Rubbish!" said Dad.
"Now we'll try Plan C.
Easy as winking
To a climber like me!"

Then he climbed up high
On the garden wall.
Guess what?
He *didn't fall*!

He gave a great leap
And he landed flat
In the crook of the tree-trunk —
Right on the cat!

The cat gave a yell
And sprang to the ground,
Pleased as Punch to be
Safe and sound.

So it's smiling and smirking,
Smug as can be,
But poor old Dad's
Still

Stuck
Up
The
Tree!

Kit Wright

Ask the children to tell you the sequence of events in their own words. Our children at Rosevern really love acting this poem. Audition for parts; select the tree (several children standing on a table), Dad, Mum and the cat.

   With older children you could write out the dialogue for each character but this is not really necessary. Children usually memorise lines very quickly. You could whisper the lines and the characters repeat them. After several rehearsals, they will be able to say their lines without prompting — or they may choose to improvise: there is no need to use the poet's exact words.

Warning

Because Dad falls down and over several times during the poem it is important to teach children how to fall without hurting themselves. It may be wise to use padded gym mats around the table's legs.

10.30–10.45   Recess

I Saw Ten Green Leaves on a Tree

I saw ten green leaves on a tree —
A magpie pecked one off with glee.
I saw   ?   (*teacher waits for response from children*)
green leaves on a tree.

I saw nine green leaves on a tree —
The west wind called "Coo-ee! Coo-ee!"
I saw   ?   green leaves on a tree.

I saw eight green leaves on a tree —
One fell off and swished "I'm free!"
I saw   ?   green leaves on a tree.

I saw seven green leaves on a tree —
But one was bitten by a bee.
I saw   ?   green leaves on a tree.

I saw six green leaves on a tree —
A silkworm ate one up for tea.
I saw   ?   green leaves on a tree.

I saw five green leaves on a tree —
But one was squashed by a possum's knee.
I saw   ?   green leaves on a tree.

I saw four green leaves on a tree
And one fell down on top of me!
I saw   ?   green leaves on a tree.

I saw three green leaves on a tree —
And one began to fall and flee.
I saw   ?   green leaves on a tree.

I saw two green leaves on a tree —
And one swirled round and round: "Whoopee!"
I saw   ?   green leaf on a tree.

I saw one green leaf on a tree
And where it is I cannot see.
SO NOW THERE'S NO GREEN LEAVES TO SEE!

This rhyme could be presented in a number of ways.
• Teacher draws a very simple tree on the chalkboard. It has

exactly ten leaves. As she reaches the third line in each
stanza (where she waits for children to supply the correct
number) she selects a child to supply the answer. If correct,
the child rubs one leaf from the tree.

- Ten children are selected as leaves. They stand out the front
of the classroom in number order: i.e. tree number one is the
first in the line, and the last tree is number ten. Get the
children to say their numbers in order.
As their number comes up, they collapse on the ground.

If you're brave enough to hear the words from one to ten yet
again, you could try singing *Ten green bottles hangin' on the
wall*; or *There were ten in the bed and the middle one said,
"Roll over . . . roll over" And they all rolled over and one fell out.
There were nine in the bed* . . .

11.10–11.30

MATHS: ORDINAL NUMBER TO TEN
Most of the children in Grade 1 will have done some ordinal
number before, but it is well worth revising and you can have
fun with the counting activities.
Before school prepare a set of large cardboard labels: first,
second, third . . . up to tenth.
Establish one-to-one correspondence by asking children to
come out the front and stand in a straight line. Touch each
person in turn as the ordinal number is pronounced and give
the children the labels.
You can play many variations on this theme. Dora Scales'
Moving Into Maths — Level 1 (Rigby) describes some of them.
E.g. Arrange the children in a line, all facing the same direction.
Distribute the ordinal number labels to other members of the
class who are sitting down. When the teacher calls an ordinal
number, the child who has the appropriate label must give it to
the child who occupies that position in the queue.

Now do Sheet 14: *Which Tree Comes First?* Children must draw
a line which connects the first label to the first tree on the page
. . . and so on until the fifth line is connected to the fifth tree.
Children could also write or trace over the labels underneath
the circles.

11.30–11.40

HUG A TREE: SENSORY AWARENESS
TEAR A TREE: ART
Go outside. Talk about trees. Talk about how huggable they are.
Allow children two or three minutes to hug their favourite tree.
(They must race back to you on a pre-arranged signal.)
Then play the game *Tear a Tree*. Give each child a piece of

51

newspaper and ask them to tear a tree from it. Display the children's trees when you come back inside.

(This is a variation of *Tear a Turtle* — see page 27.)

(This is a variation of *Tear a Turtle* — see page 27.)

11.40–12.15   STORY AND SOCIAL STUDIES

The King Who Wanted to Touch the Moon

There was once a King whose only wish was to touch the moon. He thought and thought how he could do this. In fact he could think of nothing else.

Instead of doing things that he should do, like making loud, long speeches and marching up and down on red carpets and counting out his money, he spent all of his time trying to think of a way to touch the moon. He'd lie awake all night thinking about it and when he slept he dreamt about it.

One day he called one of his carpenters and said: "I must find a way to touch the moon, so I want you to build me a tower that will reach up to the sky. After that, we'll see what we shall see."

The carpenter was too frightened to tell the King that such a tower could not be made. He would have to build the tower with wooden boxes, and there was not enough wood in the royal workshops. So he rushed around the palace pretending to make plans for the tower, but all the time he knew it could not be done.

Weeks passed and nothing happened. The King became angry and sent for his carpenter. "If you haven't built my tower in three days, I'll have your head chopped off."

Again the carpenter hurried about, hammer in hand, not knowing what to do. One day passed, then another. But on the third day the carpenter had an idea and he went to see the King.

"I'm sorry Your Majesty, but work on the tower has been held up," the carpenter said. "I have worked it all out and I see now how it can be done. I want you to get everyone to bring boxes of all sizes to the palace grounds. Tiny boxes, matchboxes, huge boxes, middle-sized boxes, giant-sized boxes. . . . Then we will have enough to build your tower to the moon."

So the King did this and thousands and millions and trillions of boxes were piled one on top of the other.

52

There were no more boxes left in the kingdom.

"It's not high enough!" roared the King when he saw the tower. "All the trees must be chopped down and made into more boxes."

At last every tree had been cut down so that never in the whole wide world had there been so many boxes.

They were piled on top of the tower which now reached up to the clouds. "I'll climb the tower first to make sure it's safe, one of the carpenters said.

"You will NOT!" shouted the King, "I'll go first." He began to climb.

He climbed and climbed to the very top and he stretched out his hand to reach the moon. Only a few more inches and he would be able to reach it.

"Bring me up one more box!" he called. There wasn't another box to be found anywhere. Nor was there a scrap of wood to make one. There wasn't a single tree left in the whole land. They had all been cut down. The King was in a fit of temper. He was so near and yet so far from touching the moon. He MUST get there.

Then he had a brilliant idea.

"Take the box from the bottom of the tower and bring it up here to me!" he called.

"What! The FIRST one?" asked the carpenters in astonishment. "You mean the box on the very bottom of the pile?"

"Of course, you dunderheads!" roared the King, "and be quick about it."

The carpenters looked at each other in fright. They knew they had to do what the king told them or their heads would be cut off.

So they shut their eyes, took a deep breath and quickly pulled out the bottom box.

You can imagine what happened.

Down came the King's tower, and somewhere under the hundreds and thousands and millions and trillions of boxes was the King.

No one knows if he was ever found, but they do know that he never touched the moon.

Norah Montgomerie

After the story, have a discussion:
Would it be possible for the world to run out of wood?
What would it be like?
Could we live without trees?
How might we make sure tha the world does not run out of trees.
(Perhaps as a discussion starter, you could ask the children to name as many things as they can which are made from wood.)

12.15–12.30	Supervise lunch
12.30–1.15	Lunch break
1.15–1.30	SONG OR CHANT

The King's Carpenter

Who built my Fath-er's house last Spring

Pe-ter the car-pen-ter ding, dong, ding

Per-son-al build-er of the king , a

laz- y , haz- y, rol - y, pol - y,

curl - y whirl - y, hurl- y, burl- y.

rare - ly, earl - y , won-der-ful clown

Pet-er the car-pen-ter ding dong ding dong

Pet-er the car-pen-ter ding dong ding.

1.30—2.15

SCIENCE: LEAF COLLECTION

Discuss leaf collection.

Ask children to find as many different kinds of leaves as they
can. Bring them inside and begin classifying: shiny, dull,
smelling, not smelling, big, little.

Talk about symmetry: veins on one side the same as veins on
the other.

Find: the leaf with the most colours, two leaves exactly alike,
leaves with holes, leaves with bumps.

If you have time, work on classification in groups. Make a leaf
chart.

Recess

ART
Before doing the art work the children could examine the leaves very carefully and discuss what qualities they would like to include in their pictures.
Our children at Rosevern enjoy the following activity:

1   Make a tree by cutting the shape of the trunk and the branches.

2   Then tear the shapes of the foliage. (Use coloured cover paper or infant squares.) Paste these shapes wherever the children want them to be. Overlapping foliage will make the picture more interesting.

3   Carefully draw the linear quality of the leaves, grass, flowers, birds and bees. The children might like to stick some real leaves to their trees if they feel this is appropriate.

You could make a mural using as many trees as possible.

If there is time during the day, or at the end, you might like to read the poem *Strange Tree* (see page 174) and then ask the children to act the story.
Or a much shorter one is this poem by Aileen Fisher, from *In the Woods, In the Meadow, In the Sky*. This could probably be incorporated in your discussion of trees (9.25–10.00).

Holes of Green

Trees are full of holes —
between the leaves, I mean.
But if you stand away enough
the holes fill up with green.

Aileen Fisher

GRADE 2

Theme: Eight

We chose EIGHT as a theme because we felt sorry for it. No
stories have eight princesses, the rainbow has only seven
colours, three princes are always searching for three quests. It's
always three wishes, three sons, six foolish fishermen, seven at
one blow, forty-seven pigs, seventeen kings, and 40,000 thieves!
WE wanted to show that there are no limits to theme
inventions: no longer need you feel dampened by the Sea,
worried by Witches or Wheat, frightened by Flight or hemmed
in by The Circus.

Let your imaginations guide you: once you get your first idea,
others will tumble out one after the other. All you have to do is
sort them and fit them to the needs and interests of the
children.

PREPARATION

1 Paper and coloured pencils to complete the story *The
Wonderful Week that had Eight Days* (pages 57–58).

2 Prepare numbers and operations signs on large cards for
Maths game:

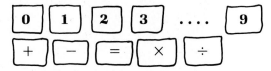

3 Prepare large labels for the characters in *The Story of Eight
People and Horace*.

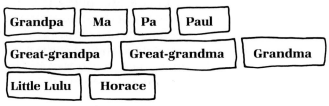

4 Write on board or chart the classification categories for the objects in the environment (see page 64).
5 Hoops and large newsprint.
6 Coloured and plain paper for the Art activity *Eight Shapes*.
or
If you are doing the *Symmetry with Eight* activity, make copies of Sheet 37, *Eight Art*.

8.55   Read the advice on page 37.

9.00—9.10   Settling in

9.10—9.50   STORYTIME AND CREATIVE WRITING

The Wonderful Week that had Eight Days

Once upon a time a King in a faraway land worked so hard that his wife, the Queen, sent him away for a relaxing holiday.

"Yippee!" cried the King, as he stuffed his crown into a suitcase. "Off I go — but I promise that I will stay away for only ONE WEEK — NOT ONE DAY LONGER!"

And the King was a man who always kept his promises.

It was a wonderful holiday.

On Monday he sailed away to a tiny island where no one was looking, hitched up his royal pants, took off his golden sandals and silken socks — and paddled and played and dived and swam all day long!

On Tuesday he watched the monkeys at the zoo for five hours, and by the end of the day he could do double somersaults better than any of them!

On Wednesday he gobbled eight chocolate sundaes and eight pies with sauce.

On Thursday, he rode on the Ferris Wheel and the Big Dipper.

On Friday he climbed the highest mountain, and floated from the top in a parachute.

On Saturday he went in the Olympic Games and won seven gold medals, and a bronze medal for hop-scotch!

On Sunday, at the end of the week, the King sadly took his crown out from his suitcase, placed it on his head, and started for home. "I wish this week could go on and on," he sighed. "I've never had so much fun,

57

and I really can't face work tomorrow. But work I must because I'm a King who ALWAYS keeps his promises."

Z A P !

Suddenly his crown fell off as he leapt in the air with an amazing idea: "Why should I go back? I'm the King. I'll make the week longer!" Then he made a proclamation (an important rule). "I, the King, do hereby declare that this week will have an extra day. So be it!" . . . .

Ask the children:

What was the name of the new eighth day of the week?

How many hours did the day contain?

What astonishing adventures did the King and all his people enjoy?

The children can then conclude the story and illustrate.

You may need to quickly retell the story, ask or suggest some ideas for new name days — and just a few examples of what the king might do.

Ideally, have a sheet of lined Grade 2 newsprint and let them know that you expect a STORY, not just a few lines. One page (with illustrations) would be satisfacatory.

9.50–10.20

MATHS WITH EIGHT

Make this number

Write the numbers from 0–9 on large cards, or sheets of paper. Give three children one card each.

Call out: Make the number 824. Children must quickly rearrange themselves to form that number:

Infinite variations can be made on this theme. E.g. have two sets of cards and two groups of three children. They race to provide the given number. The winning team is challenged by a different group, and so the game progresses.

Place Value Game

Given these three numbers $\boxed{4}$ $\boxed{8}$ and $\boxed{6}$, show me a number which has . . .

eight tens in it

eight ones (units) in it

eight hundreds in it, and so on.

58

The Equation Game

If you make a plus sign, a minus sign and an equals sign, 5 children can then be involved (or ten, if it's a race) and you can ask them to form equations for any number you wish:

If the children find it difficult to remember all five cards, you could write the equation on a board where all can see. Remember, if they find these easy, you can add the multiplication and division signs to make the game more difficult. The more that manipulation with numbers is discussed and practised by children at this age, the better!

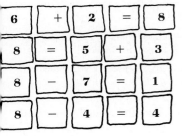

10.20–10.30

EIGHTEEN RHYMES FOR EIGHT . . . .
This activity, which involves word play and spelling, begins before morning recess and continues after the break.
In this rhyming game, the teacher says, "All the answers to these questions or statements rhyme with eight."
Give an example, "I _____ my tea."
Children respond, "ATE!"
Will we be able to get eighteen right out of eighteen?
You might need to give a clue or a hint here or there.

Eighteen Rhymes for Eight

I left it open.	gate
I _____ my breakfast.	ate
A special friend.	mate
You need it for fishing.	bait
Katie is sometimes called _____	Kate
It's on a calendar.	date
A big fair at a school.	fete
Very big or special.	great
To really dislike someone.	hate
To stay up until midnight.	late
Not crooked at all.	straight
Boring times, hanging around.	wait
We sometimes eat from a _____	plate
To blow up a rubber raft or balloon.	inflate
Holds milk bottles.	crate
Victoria or N.S.W. or Queensland is a _____	State
Very heavy.	weight
6 + 2 = _____	eight

10.30–10.45

Recess

10.50–11.15

. . . . VOCABULARY BUILDING AND SPELLING
As the children give the answers to the previous activity, write

59

the word on the board in a single column.
When the list is complete, see if the children noticed that most of the words were *a–e* words.
Which were different?
Talk about eight, eighty, eighty-eight, eighth — and how they're spelt.
Follow up queries from children who have further questions: "Why is *fete* the only word spelt that way?"
Explain that many of our words come from other countries and *fete* is a French word.

Say: now it's time for a tiny test. Look carefully once more at the words on the board.

Then give children *a–e* words, plus the word *eight*. Correct, using Cripps' method of LOOK — COVER — WRITE — CHECK.

Because of the pattern of these words, there should be little difficulty. However, when a child makes a spelling error he should LOOK at the word closely: Concentrate. Close your eyes and try to picture the word on the page. Then COVER the word so that it can't be seen. Next, WRITE the word from memory. If the word is still not correct when you CHECK it, don't just change the word, but go right back and try the LOOK, COVER, WRITE and CHECK all over again. Never copy or change a word. Write the whole thing from memory.

Other useful spelling tips, ideas and activities are given in detail in *Spelling — a Teacher's Guide*, by Colin Hudson, edited by Mary O'Toole, published by Landmark.

11.15—11.40

SONG OR CHANT: ONCE THERE WERE EIGHT FISHERMEN
(or you can call them "fisherfolk" if you prefer)
This song has a very easy-to-learn tune. If you can't read music, ask another member of staff to help you. The song is sung with much gusto, so don't worry too much if you're no Sutherland or Caruso.

Once There Were Eight Fishermen

Once there were eight fishermen
Once there were eight fishermen
Fisher fisher men men men
Fisher fisher men men men
Once there were eight fish-er-men.

Once I saw eight fish-er men Once I saw eight

fish-er men. Fish-er , fish-er men, men, men.

Fish-er, fish-er men , men, men . Once I saw eight

fish-er men.

Number One was Nicholas
Number One was Nicholas
Nickel Nickel ass, ass, ass
Nickel Nickel ass, ass, ass
Number One was Nich-o-las.

Number Two was Emily   (sing twice)
Emma Emma lee, lee, lee   (sing twice)
Number Two was Em-i-ly

Number Three was William   (sing twice)
Willy Willy yam, yam, yam   (sing twice)
Number Three was Will-i-am.

Number Four was Winifred   (sing twice)
Winnie Winnie fred, fred, fred (sing twice)
Number Four was Win-i-fred.

Number Five was Daniel   (sing twice)
Danny Danny yell, yell, yell   (sing twice)
Number Five was Dan-i-el.

Number Six was Lydia   (sing twice)
Liddy Liddy yah, yah, yah   (sing twice)
Number Six was Ly-di-a.

Number Seven was Romeo   (sing twice)
Romy Romy oh, oh, oh   (sing twice)
Number Seven was Ro-me-o.

Number Eight was Juliet   (sing twice)
Julie Julie yet, yet, yet   (sing twice)
Number Eight was Ju-li-et.

They all sailed up to Bendigo (sing twice)
Bendy Bendy go, go, go   (sing twice)
They all sailed up to Ben-di-go.

They should have gone to Amsterdam
                                                  (sing twice)

Amster Amster, sh, sh, sh   (sing twice)
They should have gone to Am-ster-dam

Oh, do not say that naughty word
                                                  (sing twice)
Naughty naughty word, word, word
                                                  (sing twice)

Do not say that naughty word!

Make up some more verses, using the names of people you know, or people you have heard about.

If you really cannot manage to sing, then say the rhyme as a chant with a very swift and vigorous rhythm — perhaps pounding your closed fists on your knees (so that the words are not drowned out).

Of course the children will chant with you.

11.40–12.00

TWO EIGHT GAMES

Buzzz with eights

Instead of saying the number eight in a counting sequence, say the word Buzzz. Anything to do with eight should be replaced by Buzzz: 8, 16, 18, 24, 28 etc. So:

1, 2, 3, 4, 5, 6, 7, Buzzz, 9, 10, 11, 12, 13, 14, 15, Buzzz, 17, Buzzz, 19, 20, 21, 22, 23, Buzzz, 25, 26, 27, Buzzz, 29, 30, 31, Buzzz. . . .

You could explore the numbers about eight on a number board. If you intend to buzzz multiples of 8 (16, 24, 32, 40, 48, 56. . .) the children may need to be helped.

Finger Eights

This is a variation of *Twelves* (see page 24). Working in pairs, children put their hands behind their backs.

On "Go!" they each hold out a certain number of fingers on one hand. If the number of fingers on the two hands comes to eight, then you have a winning pair.

12.00–12.15

HEALTH: EIGHT FINGERS AND TWO THUMBS

Before lunch, have a discussion on the necessity for clean hands before eating, and after going to the toilet. At what other times should we make sure we wash our hands? Discuss reasons. Have a fingernail inspection. (In The Olden Days, each school morning began with the teacher holding a fingernail and handkerchief inspection. Defaulters were punished.)

Activity: Trace around one of your hands; colour in your hands and nails EXACTLY as they are.

12.15–12.30

Supervise lunch

12.30–1.15

Lunch break

The Story of Eight People and Horace

Once upon a time there was a family who lived together in a little house in a wood. There was Great-grandpa, Great-grandma, Grandma, Grandpa, Ma, Pa, Paul and Little Lulu. (That's eight!) And with them lived Horace. Horace was a bear!

One day Pa went out hunting. And on the way back he was met by Great-grandma, Grandpa, Grandma, Ma, Paul and Little Lulu. And they all said, "What do you think has happened?"

And Pa said, "What has happened?"

And they said, "Horace has eaten Great-grandpa!"

And Pa was just wild, and he said, "I will kill Horace!" But they all took on so he hadn't the heart to do it.

And the next day Pa went out hunting. And on the way back he was met by Grandpa, Grandma, Ma, Paul and Little Lulu. And they all said. "What do you think has happened?"

And Pa said, "What has happened?"

And they said, "Horace has eaten Great-grandma!"

And Pa was just wild, and he said, "I will kill Horace!" But they all took on so he hadn't the heart to do it.

And the next day Pa went out hunting. And on the way back he was met by Grandma, Ma, Paul and Little Lulu. And they all said, "What do you think has happened?"

And Pa said, "What has happened?"

And they said, "Horace has eaten Grandpa!"

And Pa was just wild, and he said, "I will kill Horace!" But they all took on so he hadn't the heart to do it.

And the next day Pa went out hunting. And on the way back he was met by Ma, Paul and Little Lulu. And they all said, "What do you think has happened?"

And Pa said, "What has happened?"

And they said, "Horace has eaten Grandma!"

And Pa was just wild, and he said, "I will kill Horace!" But they all took on so he hadn't the heart to do it.

And the next day Pa went out hunting. And on the way back he was met by Paul and Little Lulu. And they both said, "What do you think has happened?"

63

And Pa said, "What has happened?"
And they said, "Horace has eaten Ma!"
And Pa was just wild, and he said, "I will kill Horace!"
But they both took on so he hadn't the heart to do it.
And the next day Pa went out hunting. And on the way back he was met by Little Lulu. And Little Lulu said, "What do you think has happened?
And Pa said, "What has happened?"
And Little Lulu said, "Horace has eaten Paul!"
And Pa was just wild, and he said, "I will kill Horace!"
But Little Lulu took on so he hadn't the heart to do it.
And the next day Pa went out hunting. And on the way back he was met by Horace. And Horace said, "What do you think has happened?
And Pa said, "What has happened?"
And Horace said, "I've eaten Little Lulu!"
And Pa was just wild, and he said, "I will kill you, Horace!" But Horace took on so he hadn't the heart to do it.
And the next day HORACE went out hunting!

If the children ask, they could act the story as a play. We have found it easier if each of the eight characters has a large sign attached to his or her front with the name of the person written in bold letters: Grandma, Little Lulu.
You will probably find that the children will join with you in retelling part or all of the story.

1.45–2.15

SCIENCE
This is a classification activity in which the children work in groups of two or three to find objects of interest in the environment.

Before going outside, discuss with the children what they can expect to find. Refer to the eight categories you have displayed on the board:

SMALL   ROUGH   SMOOTH   DEAD

BIG   BROKEN   FLAT   SHINY

Give the children hoops to place on the ground when they go outside to search for their objects. Hopefully, each child or group will be able to collect eight items of interest from the space inside the hoop to show to the rest of the class when they return to the room:

Leaves, grasses, weeds, clover, twigs, seeds, gum nuts, icy pole sticks, bubble gum paper, daisy, piece of gravel, some dirt, stone . . . .

If the children can't find eight things in one place, let them try a different area.

Once inside, groups present their classifications on large bulky newsprint.

2.15–2.30 Recess

2.30–3.10 ART AND DESIGN
Try one of these two ideas, depending on your mood and the class's artistry.

Eight Shapes
Give children a sheet of coloured paper, and a plain sheet also.

Cut eight different shapes from the coloured paper, then stick them onto the plain piece to form a picture or pattern. Lines may be added with pencils or felt pens to add finishing touches, or to connect shapes.

Symmetry with Eight
Make patterns and shapes of eight, using felt pens, paints, or coloured pencils. You could use Sheet 37, *Eight Art*, as a starting point.

3.10–3.28 PHYSICAL EDUCATION
Warm Up: Hug Tag
Assemble children in an enclosed space outside, e.g. the netball court. Call out "Eight!" Children race to form groups of eight. The first group to form eight people, shoots all sixteen arms in the air, and is declared winner.

Have several more turns, calling out different numbers — "18", "4", "$\frac{1}{2}$ of 8", "16 — 8" . . . . .

Main Game: Octopus and Shark
The playing area is preferably grassed, or, if inside, on a wooden or carpeted floor because the octopuses have to lie down and wave their tentacles around. Explain the game, emphasising the idea of the octopuses waving their tentacles (arms and legs).

Some teachers play this game with the octopuses standing up. It is more fun to lie down, but in damp weather standing up is probably healthier.

Start with 4 octopuses (i.e. 8 children).

One octopus = 2 children joined together and waving their collective arms and legs.

The remaining children are the fish, and the teacher is — of course — the shark.

65

When the teacher calls "Shark!" the fish must try to rush to the other side without being touched by any part of any octopus.

Any child who is touched becomes a new half octopus. As soon as he can, he joins up with another half, and tries to capture more fish.

The more octopuses there are, the harder it is for the fish to get to the other side. The shark can make it even more difficult by chasing the frightened fish through the waving tentacles of all the octopuses.

The game continues until there are no fish left, or until one or two agile fish are unable to be caught, and are therefore declared the winners — or The Delicacy of the Day!

3.29   Back inside. Pack up, and perhaps conclude by revising *Once There Were Eight Fishermen*.

GRADE 3

Theme: Long Nose Day

Why on earth did we choose such a theme as this? Each month at Rosevern we compile a calendar of days, dates and famous events which teachers can use as a daily source of ideas. One day we wrote *Long Nose Day* because it was Jimmy Durante's birthday. Much to our surprise, the entire Junior School — from Preps to Grade 3 — devised themes which lasted all day — and probably could have gone on even longer. Every child and teacher made a long nose, and without a shadow of a doubt the highlight was THE LONG NOSE PARADE.

PREPARATION

1 Gather materials for the Long Nose Parade. Really, the kinds of long noses produced will depend upon the materials you have available. Much of it you can collect from the classroom:

newsprint	string
newspaper	elastic
waste card	Blu-tack
kindergarten squares	

The children should have felt pens, pencils, pastels. See if you can obtain from the art room such items as cotton reels, match boxes, polystyrene bits . . .

2 Write the poem *Noses* on board or chart (see page 75)

3 Write the *Graphic Nose Quiz* on board or chart (see page 77).

4 *Smelling Stations:* This does take considerable preparation,

but it is worth it. See pages 79 to 80 for the necessary
materials and method of presentation.

or

Bring an orange and a packet of cloves (see page 80).

8.55   Read the advice given on page 37.

9.00–9.10   Settling in

9.10–9.40   STORY: THE PRINCESS OF TOMBOSO
Say something like this: It's not going to be an ordinary school
day today. That does NOT mean we are going to do no work —
far from it! It's just a different working day called *Long Nose
Day*.

Without delay (i.e. to give them no opportunity for early
morning chatter) read or tell *The Princess of Tomboso* — a long
story about a L O N G nose. At Rosevern this is the most
requested story from all children in Grades 1 to 6. (It is too long
for Preps: it takes about 20–25 minutes to read.)

The Princess of Tomboso

There was once a King who had three
sons. They did none of the things that
princes are supposed to do, but stayed
at home all day and ate their father out
of house and home. When the old King
lay dying, he called them to his bedside
and said:

"My children, I have only one thing
left to give you when I die. It is an old
bowl. When you have buried me, go to
the barn and you will find it behind the
door. Pick it up and shake it, each of you
in turn. Whatever falls out of it is your
inheritance."

Then the old man breathed his last.

It was the custom in those days to
keep the dead lying in state for a day and
a night; but the King's sons were so
anxious to see what the bowl held that
they buried their father without delay.
Then they ran to the barn and looked
behind the door. Sure enough, the bowl
was there.

The oldest son picked it up and shook
it well. Presto! A silk purse fell into the
air. Written on it in letters of gold were
these words:

EVERY TIME I OPEN WIDE
A HUNDRED FLORINS ARE INSIDE.

He opened the purse wide, and —
cling, clang! — a hundred shining florins
tumbled to the ground. He closed the
purse, opened it wide again, and found
it still full to the brim.

"It works!" he exclaimed. "I'm rich!"

The second brother was growing
impatient.

"Now it's my turn," he said.

He took the bowl, held it over his
head, and shook it. This time a silver
bugle fell out. Written on it in letters of
gold were these words:

BLOW ONE END, AND YOUR TROOPS APPEAR;
THE OTHER, AND THE FIELD IS CLEAR.

The second son lost no time. Putting the bugle to his lips, he blew a short blast. *Ta-rraa!* There in the field behind the barn stood an army of ten thousand soldiers waiting for his command.

Then he put the wide end of the bugle to his lips and blew again. Presto! In a twinkling the field was empty.

"It works!" he exclaimed. "I'm powerful!"

"Now it's my turn," said the youngest brother, whose name was Jacques.

He took the bowl and shook it. A leather belt fell out. Written on it in letters of gold were these words:

PUT ME ON AND TELL ME WHERE:
QUICK AS LIGHTNING YOU'LL BE THERE.

Jacques lost no time. Clasping the belt around his waist, he wished himself behind the barn. *Whoosh!* — and there he stood behind the barn. He wished himself back into the barn. *Whoosh!* There he was back again.

"Well, it works," he said. "Now I can travel cheap."

"And just where do you propose to go?" asked his oldest brother.

"To Tomboso," said Jacques promptly. "With my belt it will be a simple thing to visit the Princess."

His brothers looked jealous. They had heard of the Princess of Tomboso, who was as beautiful as the moon. But they had never seen her, and they didn't have a magic belt.

"You'd better look out," they told him. "She'll play some trick on you."

"Oh, no fear of that."

"Anyway, the royal guards won't even let you into the castle."

"The guards won't trouble me," said Jacques. "I'll just wish myself into the Princess' chamber, and *whoosh!* I'll be there. Farewell, my brothers."

Clasping the belt around him, he made his wish. *Whoosh!* There he

stood, in the finest room he had ever seen. And sitting on a velvet cushion by the window, eating a red apple, was the Princess of Tomboso, as beautiful as the moon.

When the Princess saw a man in her room, she gave a faint scream.

"Fair Princess," Jacques began, "do not be alarmed."

But it was too late. The Princess had fainted. Jacques sprang forward and caught her in his arms. He gazed at her in admiration. Never in his life had he seen such a lovely creature.

Presently the Princess opened her eyes.

"Are you a man from this world," she asked, "or an angel from heaven?"

"Princess, I'm a real man."

She sat up. "Then how did you arrive in my chamber? The doors are guarded, and the windows are high above the ground."

Jacques smiled modestly. "Ah, Princess, for me it was very simple. Do you see this belt I'm wearing? Well, it's no ordinary belt. I wished myself into your chamber, and *whoosh!* it brought me here."

"A magic belt? That's quite impossible," declared the Princess. "I don't believe you."

"Sweet Princess, you have something to learn. Watch me."

He wished himself down into the castle courtyard. *Whoosh!* There he was. The Princess stared down at him from her window. Then he wished himself back into her room and landed at the foot of the bed. The Princess was struck dumb with amazement.

"There," he said. "Now do you believe me?"

"What is your name?" asked the Princess.

"They call me Jacques."

"Well, Jacques, I think you are the

most outrageous liar I've ever met."

"Princess. I have told you the plain truth."

She bit her lip in thought. "Perhaps it is true for you," she said. "But would it work for me too?"

"Certainly," said Jacques.

"Prove it then. Let me see this marvellous belt of yours."

Jacques took off the belt and showed it to her. She read the words written in letters of gold: *Put me on and tell me where: quick as lightning you'll be there.* "Oh, Jacques!" she cried. "Lend it to me!"

"That I cannot do," he said firmly.

"Dear Jacques! *Please.*" And she held her arms out to him imploringly.

She looked so beautiful standing there before him that Jacques forgot his brothers' warning. He gave her the belt and watched her clasp it around her tiny waist.

"Now," she said, 'I wish to be in my father's office."

Whoosh! — and there she stood, in her father's office. The King was startled, but she gave him no explanation.

"Father!" she cried. "There is a rascal in my chamber!"

At once the King sent his guard of honor to her room. Forty soldiers seized hold of Jacques and gave him a thorough beating. When he seemed half dead, they opened a window and threw him out of the castle.

Poor Jacques landed in the ditch by the roadside and lay there unconscious for three days and nights. When at last he came to his senses, he thought:

"I cannot go home now. When my brothers hear what has happened, they will finish me off."

But he had eaten nothing for days. He was starving.

"Ah well," he said. "If I'm going to die, I might as well die at home."

When his brothers saw him stumbling up the path that evening, they knew that something must have happened to his belt. They came out of the castle shaking their fist, warning him what to expect if he came near.

But Jacques was too exhausted to care. He plodded into the castle while his brothers heaped reproaches and ridicule on his head.

"We ought to lock you up for the rest of your life," they said. "You can't be trusted on your own. Get in there under the stairs. We won't have anything more to do with you!"

For a whole month they kept him there, giving him nothing but bread and water. But one day Jacques said to his oldest brother:

"If you would lend me your purse, I could go and buy back my belt."

His brother sneered. "Do you think I would trust you with my purse after what happened to your belt?"

"But listen to my plan," said Jacques eagerly. "I'll go back to Tomboso and ask to speak to the Princess. When she asks what I want, I'll tell her the truth — that I want to buy back my belt. If she says I cannot pay for it, I shall open the purse wide and send a hundred florins rolling on the floor, *cling, clang!* If she wants more I can fill her whole room with florins, right up to the ceiling. It won't cost you anything, for the purse is never empty. In the end I'll get my belt back."

His brother grumbled, but finally he agreed.

"But I warn you," he said, "if you come back without the purse, don't expect any mercy from me."

"No fear of that," said Jacques confidently.

And so he took the purse and made his way back to Tomboso. He asked to see the Princess. When she heard who it

69

was, she had him shown up to her room. He found her eating a red apple and smiling.

"Why, hello Jacques! And what can I do for you this fine day?"

"Fair Princess, I have come to buy back my belt."

"Your belt?" The Princess pretended not to understand. "My dear Jacques, what belt are you talking about?"

"Princess, I'll pay you a good price for it."

She laughed. "A young lad like you couldn't possibly afford to buy a valuable belt."

"I can fill this room with pieces of gold," said Jacques.

"How you boast, Jacques! Why, even my father the King hasn't enough gold florins to fill this room."

"I can fill it to the ceiling," said Jacques. "For me it's no trick at all."

The Princess shook her head. "Ah, Jacques, you never change. One simply can't believe a word you say."

"Very well, you shall see," said Jacques. "I have a little silk purse in my pocket. Open it wide, and a hundred florins tumble out. Open it wide again, and there are a hundred more."

He took the purse from his pocket and opened it wide, and — *cling, clang!* — a hundred shining florins fell to the floor. The Princess stared at them with round eyes.

"There," he said. "Now do you believe me?"

"Ah," she breathed. "With a purse like that, you can buy back any belt you like. But how can I be sure it will go on giving florins?"

"Look," said Jacques, "it's still full." And — *cling, clang!* — he spilled another hundred gold pieces on the floor.

"Oh!" said the Princess. "Would it do that for me, too?"

"Certainly."

"Please let me try!"

"That I cannot do," said Jacques firmly.

"Dear Jacques! *Please.*" And she held out her arms as if to embrace him. She looked so beautiful that he forgot his resolutions and gave her the purse.

But she was still wearing the magic belt. At once she wished herself into her father's office. *Whoosh!*

The King looked up from his desk. "Terrible draught in here," he said. "Oh, it's you, my dear. What's the matter now?"

"Quick, Father! That rascal has come back to insult me."

The King's soldiers rushed to her room, captured Jacques, beat him nearly to death, and flung him out of the window.

For five days and nights he lay in the ditch unconscious. Finally he awoke and groaned.

"This time it's all over," he thought. "If I go back home, my brothers will finish me off for certain."

But he was so hungry that he had no choice. Once again he trudged wearily home.

His brothers had been searching for him for days. When they saw him approach, bruised and mud-stained, a pitiful sight, they guessed what had happened. They shook their sticks in the air, warning him what to expect if he came nearer. But poor Jacques didn't care. He stumbled into the castle and his brothers gave him another beating. Then they shut him up under the stairs with a jug of water and a bone to gnaw.

"That's all you'll get from us," they said. "When you finish that, there won't be any more."

For a whole month he stayed there, growing thinner and thinner. Then one day he spoke to his second brother, the one who had the silver bugle.

"If you lend it to me," said Jacques, "I'll go and get back the belt and the purse."

His brother sneered. "Do you think I would trust my bugle to a nitwit like you? You would only let it be stolen too."

"But I have a better plan. This time I won't even go to the Princess' room, so she won't have a chance to steal the bugle. I'll wait at the city gates until the King and the Princess drive out in their royal carriage. Then I'll seize the bridle, stop the horses, and command the Princess to return the belt and the purse, or else I'll besiege the city with my army and put the whole population to the sword."

His brother grumbled but finally agreed.

And so with the bugle under his arm Jacques once more took the road to Tomboso. By next morning he was ready, standing at the gates of the city. When the royal carriage came into sight, he blew the silver bugle. *Ta-rraa!* There stood an army of ten thousand men.

"General, we await your orders."

"Men," said Jacques, "surround the city."

The King of Tomboso was astonished to see so many soldiers, and the Princess was so frightened that she dropped the red apple she was eating. But when she saw who ran forward to hold the bridle of the horses, she smiled.

"So it's you again, Jacques! And what are you up to this time?"

"Fair Princess," said Jacques sternly, "if you do not return my belongings, I will give orders to sack the town."

"Good heavens!" cried the Princess. "This sounds serious. Of course I'll give everything back to you. I wasn't going to keep them anyway. But tell me first, brave general, where did you enlist this great army?"

"Fair lady, to raise an army like this is a very simple thing for me."

"A simple thing?" said the Princess. "Really, I can't believe that."

"Very well," said Jacques, "I'll tell you how it's done. Do you see this silver bugle? If I blow it at one end, ten thousand soldiers appear. Blow the other end, and they all vanish."

The Princess laughed. "A bugle does all that? Really, Jacques, I think you must be the prince of liars."

He blew the bugle at the wide end. Presto! In a twinkling the field was empty. Then he blew the other end and the whole army reappeared, ready to attack the town.

"Stop, stop!" cried the Princess. "I shall give you back what you asked for. But tell me, does the bugle obey you alone?"

"Why, no," said Jacques. "It obeys whoever blows it."

She unclasped the belt from her waist and pulled out the purse. But before handing them over to him, she said:

"What a wonderful bugle! May I try blowing it, just once?"

Jacques hesitated.

The Princess gave him an enchanting smile. "Dear Jacques," she said. "*Please.*"

"Can I trust you this time?" he demanded.

"I give you my word," said the Princess. "The word of Tomboso. If the bugle obeys me too, I shall return your belt and your purse."

And so poor Jacques forgot his promise and gave her the bugle. As soon as she had it she blew into the wide end. Presto! In a twinkling Jacques' army vanished. Then she blew at the other end. *Ta-rraa!* A new army appeared.

"Princess, we await your orders."

"Take this scoundrel," said the Princess, "and march over his body till he is seven times dead."

Two soldiers held Jacques down. Then the whole army marched over him until he was pounded flat into the ground.

For seven days and seven nights Jacques lay there without moving. But he must have had at least seven lives, for at last one morning he woke.

"This really is the end," he groaned. "I can never go home now."

Slowly he pulled himself out of the ground. His legs were so weak that he could hardly stand. Falling every few yards, he staggered away from Tomboso, following a little footpath that wound into the woods. He came to a marsh full of big green rushes, and there he lost the path. Several times he nearly drowned. Finally he fell exhausted in the hot sunshine at the edge of a clearing.

"Well," he thought, "I'll try to reach that apple tree. At least I'll be able to die in the shade."

Dragging himself along the ground, he got as far as the apple tree. Its branches were so laden with ripe shining fruit that they bent down within his reach. Nearby there was another tree, weighed down with plums.

"It must be an old orchard," said Jacques to himself. "I don't think I'll die just yet — not until I've had a little refreshment."

He ate one apple and a strange thing happened. His nose began to feel heavy, as if it was ready to drop off. He ate another, and his head began to bend forward with the weight. He ate a third apple, and by this time his nose had grown so long that it touched the ground.

"Thunderation!" cried Jacques. "Am I going to die with a nose like an elephant?"

He crawled on all fours to the plum tree. His nose was so heavy that he could not stand up. Rolling on his back, he kicked at the lowest branch. Plums fell all around him.

"Well" he thought, "they can't be any worse."

He ate one. It tasted sweet and juicy, and he felt better immediately. He ate another. Better still — now he could lift his head. At each mouthful he felt his nose shrinking, until by the time he had eaten three plums it was the finest nose you have ever seen.

"Let me see now. Eat apples, and your nose grows. Eat plums, and it shrinks. And I know someone who is very fond of fruit. Oho! My affairs are mending!"

Cheerfully he made his way back to the marsh where he cut down some rushes and plaited himself two baskets. The first he filled with apples, the second with plums. Then he set out toward Tomboso again.

In front of the castle he walked up and down, shouting like a peddler:

"Apples for sale! Fresh apples!"

The Princess, who was very fond of apples, sent a servant downstairs to buy some. When she saw how delicious the fruit looked, she didn't worry about spoiling her dinner but began eating right away. She soon felt strange. She tried to stand up and fell forward on her face. Horrified, she stood up again and began running toward her bed. This time she tripped over her nose!

Feeling very sick indeed, she took to her bed and sent for the doctor. When he arrived she hid her face in the pillows so that he wouldn't see her nose. He felt her pulse and shook his head.

"Your Highness," he said, "this is an odd kind of illness. You have no sign of a fever and your pulse is normal. Let me see your tongue."

The Princess shrieked so loudly that her servants came running.

"This doctor has insulted me!"

They threw the doctor out.

Jacques, who was waiting outside, said: "Good doctor, I think I can cure her. Be kind enough to lend me your cloak and your square cap. I will pay you well."

"No need to pay me," panted the doctor. "I've had enough of Tomboso."

And flinging his cloak and cap at Jacques, he ran off.

Jacques picked up his basket of plums, which he had covered with green leaves and hidden by the roadside. Wearing the doctor's cap and gown and a very serious expression, and carrying the basket on his arm, he asked to be admitted to the castle. He was led to the Princess' room.

"It's another doctor," said the maid to the Princess. "This one looks like a medicine man. He's got no little black bag, only a basket of herbs."

"Show him in."

Jacques entered. He could not see the Princess' face, for she kept it hidden among her pillows.

"Your Highness," he said, 'how can I find out what is wrong with you if you won't let me see your tongue?"

She raised her head to shout for the servants. But Jacques seized her shoulders and turned her face up.

"Ah," he said. "So that's it! Why, Princess, you have a monster of a nose!"

"He's insulting me!" she shouted.

"Do you want to have me thrown out," asked Jacques, "or do you want to be cured?"

The Princess stopped shrieking. "Oh — can you cure me?"

Jacques took a plum from his basket. "Eat this," he said, "and we shall see."

The Princess ate the plum. Her nose grew a few inches shorter. She began to feel better. "Oh, you are a good doctor! Let me have another one."

"Not just yet." Jacques put down the basket and touched his fingers together. "You have another disease which we must cure first."

The Princess was astonished. "Another disease? What is that?"

"A naughty habit of taking things that don't belong to you."

"Why, Doctor, who could have told you a story like that?"

"Never mind how I know," said Jacques. "It is true, is it not?"

"Well," admitted the Princess, "I do happen to have a small belt here, but it's the merest trifle, hardly worth mentioning."

"Let me have that belt. Otherwise I am afraid I can do nothing for you."

"Certainly not," said the Princess. "I refuse to part with it."

"Very well. In that case I shall leave you here — with your nose." And Jacques picked up his basket, ready to depart.

"Wait, Doctor!" cried the Princess. She unclasped the belt and gave it to him. "Here it is. Now will you cure my nose?"

Jacques clasped the belt securely around his waist. "Your Highness, are you sure there isn't some other trifle that doesn't belong to you?"

"No, nothing else . . . well, only a little purse."

"Let me have that little purse, Your Highness."

"No. I would rather die than part with it."

"Very well," said Jacques. "If that is your decision, I shall leave you. Good day, Princess."

"Wait," said the Princess. "Here it is." And she gave him the purse. "Now will you cure my nose?"

"Not yet," said Jacques. "I think there is still one thing left."

"Oh, there is only a little bugle that I received from a certain young man. I really don't see what importance it could have."

"Nevertheless you must give it up. I must have the bugle too. Otherwise I cannot cure you completely."

The Princess burst into tears, but finally she had to give up the bugle. Then Jacques gave her plums to eat until her nose shrank. When he stopped, it was a very handsome nose, but it was

73

exactly one foot long.

The Princess protested. "Surely you don't call this a complete cure?"

"It is more than you deserve," said Jacques. Stepping back, he took off his doctor's cap and gown and bowed to her. When she recognized him, she gave a little scream.

"Yes," he said, "it is Jacques. You have treated me very badly, Princess."

She held out her arms. "Oh, Jacques, forgive me! Come, let me kiss you and make up for everything."

"No, thank you," said Jacques, picking up his basket. "I really don't care to kiss a Princess with a nose like yours. From now on, you know, they will call you the Princess with the Twelve-Inch Nose. Farewell, Your Highness!"

Since he was now wearing his belt again, he had only to wish himself home, and *whoosh!* — there he was. This time you may be sure that his brothers welcomed him with open arms. They praised his cleverness in recovering the belt and the purse and the bugle, and Jacques for his part resolved that he had learned his lesson. The three of them lived quite happily ever afterward, and Jacques never went near Tomboso again.

9.40–9.50

Brainstorm: discuss with the children what kinds of things might happen on a long nose day.

You could add these ideas: a competition to see who has the keenest sense of smell, some smelly spelling, some smelldiferous sums, some polluted poems, some huffing and puffing, some birds and beaks.

Tell them about the Long Nose Parade, to be held at noon, and suggest that they may like to begin making a long nose to be worn at the Parade.

9.50–10.30

ART: MAKING NOSES

If there are no other materials in the school or the classroom, noses can be made from paper (newsprint, newspaper, waste card, kindergarten squares) decorated with oil pastels or feltpens, and when completed, held onto the face by hand, or attached in some other way such as string, elastic, Blu-tack. The noses would be more durable, however, if you could plead or beg from the art room some stronger paper — cover paper, thin card, or whatever else is available. Don't limit yourself to a paper proboscis: ask the children for other ways of nose-making — decorating a cotton reel, half a ping-pong ball, match box nose, banana nose or a leaf-twig-bark nose.

Walk around, admiring and helping, but try to find some time to make your own nose. (One teacher used an ice-cream cone attached to her face by some elastic. Another made a long paper beak and invited children to use it for nosey graffiti.)

Before recess, display noses on shelf, even if they are not completed. The Nose Parade will be held at noon so if children work particularly well during the morning, you could allow them extra time to complete their efforts.

10.30–10.45	Recess

10.45–11.20   CALLIGRAPHY
As a settling activity, children copy the poem from the board in
their most careful and beautiful writing. Use decorative borders,
and perhaps some illustrations, if there is time.

Noses

I looked in the mirror
and looked at my nose:
it's the funniest thing,
the way it grows
stuck right out where all of it shows
with two little holes where the breathing goes.
I looked in the mirror
and saw it there,
the end of my chin
and the start of my hair
and between there isn't much space to spare
with my nose, like a handle, sticking there.
If ever you want
to giggle and shout
and can't think of what
to do it about,
just look in the mirror and then, no doubt,
you'll see how funny *your* nose sticks out!

Aileen Fisher

When most children have completed their work, each row or
table comes to the front for the admiration of the other class
members.

11.20–11.40   NOSE SPELLING
Ask children to build up a list — anything whatsoever to do
with the sense of smell:
> breathing, perfume, odours, sniff, smell, nose, cold, sniffle,
> sneeze, breath, breathe, puff, asthma, nostril, scent, whiff,
> aroma, fume, inhale, exhale, fragrant, reek.

Go over the list with the children. Which words are too easy for
Grade 3; which ones are too hard? Select about fifteen
(including one or two easy and more difficult ones).
Use these words for the *Smelling Spelling Test*.

Correct words, using the LOOK, COVER, WRITE and CHECK method (described on page 60).

Special Awards could be made for the test, e.g. First Prize — three big, deep breaths, or a petal from a daisy . . . whatever you think.

11.40–12.00

TWO OPTIONS

i Children draw profiles of other class members' noses. Pin on display board. See if others can guess whose noses are displayed.

ii Complete noses for the Parade.

12.00–12.15+

THE NOSE PARADE

Improvise a catwalk — perhaps a table with a chair on either side.

Each entrant is introduced by the M.C. (the teacher) or by two M.C.s who alternate. The child M.C. would need to be a fluent, confident and humorous child. Keep things moving quickly. E.g. "Tony's nose is a delicate shade of green, enhanced by fashionable orange spots. The lack of nostrils is highly innovative and could be very useful in malodorous moments."

12.15–12.30

Supervise lunch. (If the Parade is not finished, children could continue in this time, while eating lunch.)

12.30–1.15

Lunch break

1.15–1.55

MATHS: GRAPHIC NOSING

Divide the grade into four or five groups (about seven in each group is ideal).

Ask the children how long they think they can hold their breath. They will give interesting answers ranging from 5 minutes to 5 seconds.

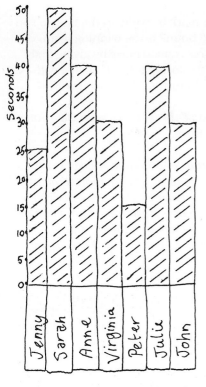

Write on the board next to their names the first five guesses, e.g. Jenny says 10 seconds.
Virginia says 1 hour.
Now see how long the children can *really* hold their breath. List all the children's names on the board in their groups.
Group 1 children stand up, the other children watch the wall clock. On the signal GO! children take a deep breath and hold their noses. When their breaths run out they sit down and their times are recorded by chosen judges, with the teacher as supervisor. A recorder places the scores on the board. For a group of seven or eight children, this process will take only a few minutes.
When all the groups have had their turns and the times are recorded, show the children how to graph the results.

The children then make graphs of their own group's efforts, and complete the *Graphic Nose Quiz* (which should be written on the board or on a chart).

Graphic Nose Quiz
1 Who held their breath longest?
2 Who held their breath for the least time?
3 By how many seconds did the winner beat the runner-up?
4 Select one member from your group. Look at his or her score. How many more seconds to reach 1½ minutes?
5 Which person held his or her breath nearest to 30 seconds?
6 Which person held his or her breath nearest to 10 seconds?
7 How many people in your group held their breath for longer than 25 seconds?
8 What is the total time of all the people in your group?
Correct and discuss the graph work and the quiz. Perhaps you might establish a winner by seeing which group had the highest total in minutes and seconds.

1.55–2.15

ORAL CLOZE COMPETITION
This is a listening/thinking/quick response comprehension activity. Read a passage, in this case part of the story of Pinocchio. At frequent intervals stop, and the children have to guess which word comes next. First hand up is given first guess; after that it is boy-girl-boy-girl (alternate turns) until someone comes up with the answer. This is a competition. We find it easier to use Girls/Boys, although many of our colleagues prefer Groups or Houses.

When a correct guess is made a mark is made on the board. The first team to gain ten (or twenty) points is the winning team. You can make sure that the scores remain close by giving first guess at the easiest answers to the losing team. If challenged, say "His hand was up first, and no further discussion will be entered into!"

We have chosen *Pinocchio* because this is Long Nose Day, but you could use any piece of literature.

Once upon a . . . . . . [pause] (***time*** — *everyone will get this!*) there was . . . . [pause] (***a***) piece of . . . . . . (*children might answer: timber? — no; cake? — no; material? — no; wood? YES!*)

It was not the . . . . . . (*the answer is **best**, but if after eight or nine guesses, the children can't get it, say the word and continue the story. No one scores.*) piece of wood, but just an . . . . . . (*ordinary*) piece, such as we . . . . . . (*use*) to kindle a . . . . . . (*fire*) and warm our . . . . . . (*rooms*) during the long, cold . . . . . . (*Winter*).

One fine . . . . . . (*day*) this piece . . . . . . (*of*) wood happened to be . . . . . . (*in*) the shop of an old . . . . . . (*carpenter*) whose name . . . . . . (*was*) Mr. Antonio, but everyone called . . . . . . (*him*) Mr. Cherry, because the end of his . . . . . . (*nose*) was always . . . . . . (*red*) and shiny like a ripe . . . . . . (*cherry*).

As soon as Mr. Cherry . . . . . . (*saw*) this piece of . . . . . . (*wood*), he was very . . . . . . (*pleased*). He clapped his . . . . . . (*hands*) together and . . . . . . (*said*), "This has come in the nick of . . . . . . (*time*). It is just what I . . . . . . (*need*) to make a . . . . . . (*leg*) for my little . . . . . . (*table*).

Note: In educationally sound Cloze exercises, close answers are acceptable, even welcomed. In this method, however, the children have to guess the author's exact word, so that the game will be perfectly fair and above board.

At Rosevern, we have been amazed to find how popular this activity is with all classes — even with Grade 1 (of course, you must choose material suitable for the age level of the class).

2.15–2.30	Recess
2.30–3.10	THE SENSE OF SMELL: DISCUSSION AND WRITING

Discuss what is good and bad about the sense of smell. If you had to lose one of your senses (Sight, Touch, Hearing, Taste, Smell) which one would you choose? Which sense is the most important to you?

Then focus the discussion on the sense of smell. How important is it to you? Remember that if you can't smell, you can't taste.

List your favorite smells.

Talk about the dangers if you weren't able to smell:

You couldn't smell smoke if your house was burning down.

You couldn't tell if the milk was "off".

You wouldn't know if there was a gas leak.

You couldn't identify clear liquids in bottles without labels —
water, metho, turps, lemonade, mineral water.

Write a story called **The Smell Stealers** in which a wicked
group invents a secret formula which is able to get rid of every
smell on earth. How do they plan their attack? Does it succeed?
How do you defeat them in the end?

3.10—3.30

SMELLING STATIONS

We have devised some ideas for different lessons for this time.
We prefer the *Smelling Stations*, but if you are called to a grade
and have had no time to prepare, this lesson would be
impossible.

If you DO have time, we can assure you that all the preparation
time is well and truly worth it.

We want to present the children with a number of different
smells to identify. The problem is to allow them to smell the
substance, without seeing what it is.

One method is to use small bags made from very fine material
or gauze. Fill the inside and staple round the edges if you can't
sew.

We tried using emptied out tea bags (unused) but this was not
entirely satisfactory. It was hard to disguise the smell of the tea
leaves, and we could see what was in some of the bags.

Or you could collect small yoghurt containers.

Use doubled over tissues and elastic bands for covers.

Fill each bag, bottle or other container with substances which
have a distinctive smell. Here are some, but you can add your
own.

smelly cheese	pepper
coffee	lavender
crushed eucalypt leaves	rose petals
crushed garlic	grass
onion pieces	nail polish remover
perfumed soap	(impregnate a piece of
chocolate	absorbent material)
bubblegum (freshly chewed)	beer (as for polish remover)
toothpaste	sawdust
leather	baby powder (as for
Vicks VapoRub	polish remover)
the toe of a smelly sock	ammonia/White King (as
tobacco	for polish remover)

SMELLS
1. sawdust
2.
3. garlic
4.
5. coffee
6. grass
7. smelly socks
8.
9. toothpaste
10. pepper
11. peanuts

Select about sixteen substances, and make smelling stations at various places in the room. Number each bag or bottle.

Children make their own scoring sheets by numbering lines on their jotters or books from 1–16. They smell the substances (NO TOUCHING OR LOOKING) and enter their guesses beside the appropriate number.

To avoid overcrowding, children can do any bag in any order. Try not to have more than two or three people at any station at any one time.

Just before the bell, sit the children down and have them call out their answers. Which ones were always guessed correctly? Which ones were hard to identify?

Who is the classroom's Champion Sniffer?

Alternative Lesson Ideas

If you haven't had time to prepare for this lesson you could:

1 Make up your own idea. Perhaps discuss rubbish bins, tips and dumps. What could be found there?

2 Read a selection from *Bottersnikes and Gumbles*, by S. Wakefield (Collins).

3 Discuss air pollution, and make a poster — along the *Keep Australia Beautiful* line. Children make up their own slogans "It's On The Nose!" . . . .

4 Again, if you had time to bring along an orange and a packet of cloves, the class could make a **pomander**. The idea is to completely cover the orange with cloves. Pass the orange around the room. Each child quickly pokes one clove into the orange and passes it to the next person.

The record time for making a pomander at Rosevern is 7 minutes 42 seconds.

Hang the pomander in the classroom to help keep the air fresh. (Some people hang them in wardrobes and cupboards.)

GRADE 4

Theme: Puddins

PREPARATION

1 If possible, bring a copy of Norman Lindsay's *The Magic Pudding.*

2 Make copies of Sheet 6, *The Surprise Birthday Party.*

3 Make copies of Sheet 18, *Grandpa's Shortbread.*

4 Place on board the columns for the *Toothless Wonder Quiz* (see page 88).

5 Hoops and about thirty bean bags.

6 For *potato printing*: several large potatoes, knives and plates, paper, paint, brushes and water. Prepare the paint and brushes at afternoon recess.

8.55 Read the advice given on page 37.

9.00–9.10 Settling in

9.10–9.15 Explain the theme of the day, *Puddins*, which is a tribute to Norman Lindsay's famous Australian book *The Magic Pudding*. Actually, the REAL theme is **food**.

Most of the children will be too young to appreciate the humour of *The Magic Pudding*, but you could tell them a little about it — how the Puddin always grows back to his normal size, no matter how much of him is eaten. If you can find a copy of the book, show the children pictures of the main characters — Bunyip Bluegum, Bill Barnacle, Sam Sawnoff and — of course — the Puddin. This book is an important part of Australia's literary heritage.

9.15–9.35 FUN WITH RHYME

A Hungry Story

I'm so hungry I could eat anything.
    ANYthing?
    How about some chocolate noodles?
That sounds good. Give me oodles.
    What about some nice fried cork?
That's for me! Got a fork?
    I also have a hard-boiled brick.
I'll eat it if it's good and thick.
    And how about this muddy goop?
Put a spoonful in my soup.
    Look! Here's a fresh hot icicle!
I'll eat that on my bicycle!
    Would you like some chopped-up junk?
Wow! I'd like a great big hunk.
    How about a glass of ink?
Yes, I think I'd like a drink.
    Here's some purple gooey-gummy.
That doesn't sound so very yummy.
    Would you like a little glop?
Not too much, please — just a drop.
    How about some turnip paste?

I think I only want a taste.
    What about some buttered hay?
I don't think so, not today.
    Isn't that the dinner bell?
Excuse me, please: I don't feel well.

Ruth B. Gross

Read this poem in two voices, or choose a very good reader to
read the response lines (in italics). Then ask if any others would
like a turn, perhaps changing or adding a few lines of their own.
Then make up some different lines and wait for responses.
Remember, the children must respond with a rhyming reaction
to your line.
I'm so hungry. . . .
    WHAT ABOUT A NICE FRESH SLUG?
    Children might respond:
    Don't be daft — I'm not a mug!
    Yes please — it tastes good — glug, glug, UGH!
    It could be nice served in a jug.

Ask children to work in pairs on jotter or notepaper, to see if
they can make up one or two hungry rhymes of their own to
share with the class.

HERE'S SOME SCONES MADE OUT OF MUD.

_____

NEXT WE'LL HAVE A DRINK OF SLIME.

_____

WHAT ABOUT CRUNCHY CHALK ON TOAST?

_____

OH LOOK AT THESE DELICIOUS ANTS!

_____

9.35–10.20

MATHS: GRAPHING
Discuss foods we like and those we dislike.
Make a list of eight of the children's most popular foods and
eight of their most unpopular. List these in two columns on
the board.

Popular foods	Unpopular foods
Icecream	Pumpkin
Lollies	Silver beet
Sausage rolls	Stew
Fish and chips	Egg sandwiches

82

McDonalds	Smelly cheese
Cakes	Smoked fish
Chicken	Porridge
Twisties	Brussels sprouts

The children vote for their favourite food. The child nominating a food must vote for it, and only one vote is allowed for each child.

Tally up scores by putting one stroke for each vote.

Ice-cream ### //

Lollies //

Twisties ///

Ask the question: How could we make a picture graph to show which is the most popular food in our grade? Talk about bar graphs. (This is an extension of work described in the Grade 3 theme.)

Work on the board with the children. Revise how to construct a bar graph. Talk about the use of symbols to represent each food.

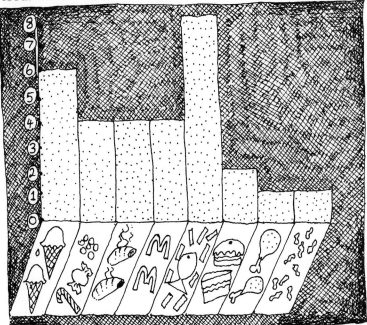

Discuss which is the most popular food and how we can tell. Now let the children construct their own graph for the most unpopular food. Remind them that one line represents one vote. Talk about the kind of symbols they will use for the most unpopular foods.

Try to make time (before recess) to have a brief discussion (or display) of the children's findings.

10.20–10.25	CHANT A really delicious play-time entreé would be to read the tongue-twisty rhyme: *Yellow butter* by Mary Ann Hoberman. We discovered this in an excellent collection — *Poems for Fun* (Beaver Books).

Yellow butter

Yellow butter purple jelly red jam black bread

Spread it thick
Say it quick

Yellow butter purple jelly red jam black bread

Spread it thicker
Say it quicker

Yellow butter purple jelly red jam black bread

Now repeat it
While you eat it

Yellow butter purple jelly red jam black bread

Don't talk
With your mouth full!

Mary Ann Hoberman

Encourage the children to learn the rhyme as quickly as possible.
The trick (which children really love) is to allow them to call out loudly the last two lines:
    Don't talk
    With your mouth full!

10.25–10.30	Continue this rhyme if children are enjoying themselves. Or try a few more lines to add to the *Hungry Story*, mentioned earlier.
10.30–10.45	Recess
10.45–11.00	COMPREHENSION: THE SURPRISE BIRTHDAY PARTY Sheet 6 is a piece of writing which is riddled with mistakes. Children take a sheet and underline all the errors. This could also be an oral language activity: read the piece several times, and then ask the children to tell you the mistakes they noticed.

11.00–11.45	MATHS: GRANDPA'S SHORT BREAD

Give out Sheet 18 and discuss shortbread. Talk about the measurements needed: grams in a kilogram, how long shortbread is cooked, etc. Complete the sheet.

When the children have finished, discuss and correct. Tell the children to keep their sheets: they may like to take them home and ask their parents to help them make some shortbread when they have time. Perhaps they will find a different recipe at home. What are the main differences?

If you are in the grade for more than one day, you could make the shortbread with the children. This would ensure the popularity of this maths lesson.

(Note: the idea for Grandpa's shortbread is taken from Rigby *Moving Into Maths* Level 4 (Irons and Scales), which is full of excellent maths ideas.)

11.45–12.15	SMORGASBORD

Choose one or more of these pre-lunch activities.

Shortnin' bread

This song would fit in very well at this time.

Shortnin' bread is a kind of corn bread made with strips of bacon. The *short* in Grandpa's shortbread is the fat or shortening — in this case butter.

Three little ba-bies ly-in' in bed, Two were sick and the oth-er 'most dead. Sent for the doc-tor and the doc-tor said, Give those ba-bies some short-nin' bread.' Mam-my's lit-tle ba-by loves short-nin', short-nin', Mam-my's lit-tle ba-by loves Short-nin' bread.

Mam-my's lit-tle ba-by loves short-nin', short-nin', Mam-my's lit-tle ba-by loves short-nin' bread

Food words
How have people from other countries contributed to our diet? Build up a list or a chart of foods which came from other countries. Have a short spelling test — children who do well might one day be great linguists — or champion gourmets!

chili con carne	omelette
crepe	pita
dim sim	pizza
felafel	sauerkraut
fetta cheese	shish kebab
gelati	souvlaki
gazpacho	spaghetti
hamburger	sukiyaki
liverwurst	taboule
nasi goreng	taco

Spaghetti
Read the poem by Shel Silversteen to the class.
(Most of the children at Rosevern adore spaghetti — we suspect that the passion is universal.)

Spaghetti

Spaghetti, spaghetti, all over the place,
Up to my elbows — up to my face,
Over the carpet and under the chairs,
Into the hammock and wound round the stairs,
Filling the bathtub and covering the desk,
Making the sofa a mad mushy mess.

The party is ruined, I'm terribly worried,
The guests have all left (unless they're all buried).
I told them, "Bring presents." I said, "Throw confetti."
I guess they heard wrong
'Cause they all threw spaghetti!

Shel Silverstein

Healthy lunches
What do the children think they will have in their lunches today? Is it good? Will they enjoy it? Talk about a balanced diet. Will all the children eat every bit of their lunches? If you think it

86

is appropriate, you could mention people from poverty-stricken countries. What do they eat? Can they be helped?

The main emphasis should be on their own lunches.

If they have chips, cakes, lollies, it is important that there is a balance — vegetables, fruit, cheese — at some other time during the day.

The children could then get out their lunches a bit early and see if they guessed the contents correctly.

12.15–12.30   Supervise lunch

12.30–1.15   Lunch break

1.15–1.20   POEM
Look the children straight in the eyes, then read in a bossy voice: (until you get to the last two lines!)

Toothpaste

Who's been at the toothpaste?
I know some of you do it right
and you squeeze the tube from the bottom
and you roll up the tube as it gets used up,
don't you?

But somebody
somebody here —
you know who you are
you dig your thumb in
anywhere, anyhow
and you've turned that tube of toothpaste
into a squashed sock.
You've made it so hard to use
it's like trying to get toothpaste
out of a packet of nuts.

You know who you are.
I won't ask you to come out here now
but you know who you are.

And then you went and left the top off, didn't you?
So the toothpaste turned to cement.

People who do things like that should . . .
you should be ashamed of yourself.

I am.

Michael Rosen

87

TEETH

Hold a teeth inspection. How many fillings?

Children peer inside each other's mouths and count.

Tell them about SWISH AND SWALLOW: If it is impossible to clean your teeth every time you eat something, always take a mouthful of water and swish the water vigorously around your mouth.

Then swallow the water — do not spit it at any anyone else!

Strips of celery or carrot strips work well too.

Now do the **Toothless Wonder Quiz**.

There are ten questions (but you can add, delete or make up better questions if you wish). Read each question, allowing enough time for the children to tick the appropriate column in a grid they have drawn up for themselves.

Toothless wonder quiz	
Agree	Disagree
1	
2	
3	
4	
5	

1 Chewing gum is good for your teeth.
2 You should scrub your teeth with a hard toothbrush.
3 The best time to brush your teeth is first thing in the morning.
4 Crunchy vegetables are good for your teeth.
5 You may as well wait until your tooth aches before you go to the dentist.
6 Is dental floss of any value or use?
7 Always rinse your mouth out after using toothpaste.
8 Banana flavoured toothpaste is best.
9 It's good to pull out baby teeth as soon as possible so that your second teeth can grow faster.
10 If a tooth is left in Coke for a time some of it will dissolve.

PHYSICAL EDUCATION

Bean bag activities.

Before you begin, hold up bean bags, rattle them, sniff them, pinch them. What is really inside those bags? Could you eat them?

a Divide class into groups. Practise throwing and catching bean bags.

b Choose several teams. Each child attempts to throw a bean bag into his group's hoop.

c All children are at one end, behind a line. If there are thirty children, place twenty-nine bean bags in a hoop. If there are thirty-two children, place thirty-one . . .

On a signal from the teacher, children race for a bean bag. The child who misses out is eliminated from the game. Continue until there is only one bean bag in the hoop, and two children. Who is the final winner?

Skipping song

Salt, Mustard, Vinegar, Pepper

Salt, Mustard, Vinegar, Pepper,
French almond rock,
Bread and butter for your supper
That's all mother's got.
Fish and chips and coca cola,
Put them in a pan,
Irish stew and ice cream soda,
We'll eat all we can.

Salt, Mustard, Vinegar, Pepper,
French almond rock,
Bread and butter for your supper
That's all mother's got.
Eggs and bacon, salted herring,
Put them in a pot,
Pickled onions, apple pudding,
We will eat the lot.

Salt, Mustard, Vinegar, Pepper,
Pig's head and trout,
Bread and butter for your supper
O-U-T spells out.

Read this traditional old rhyme in a definite skipping rhythm.
We usually say something like this:
We want you to skip in time to the rhythm of these words. You
will need to skip fairly lightly so that you can hear the words. If
I speak quickly — you must skip quickly; if I slow down, so
must you. Please skip up and down in the same place.
If there are any complaints about skipping being a sissy game,
remind them that all footballers and most athletes use skipping
as a very good exercise for keeping fit.

| 2.15–2.30 | Recess |
| 2.30–2.50 | STORY |

The Thin King and the Fat Cook

Once upon a time there was a very fat King who said to
his very thin cook, "Bake me a cake! The lightest,
nicest, scrumpiest cake you've ever made."

So the cook got a big bowl and two dozen eggs and some butter and five pounds of flour and a pound of yeast.

He mixed the flour and the eggs and the butter in the big bowl, then put in the yeast. Then he lit the gas and when the oven was hot he put the cake in.

Soon there was a lovely smell of baking cake, and the King came running in.

"My, my!" he said. "What a lovely smell. I'm sure it's going to be a delicious cake, cook."

"Ah yes, Your Majesty," said the cook. "And it's going to be the lightest cake in the world, I put in a whole pound of yeast to make it rise."

"That's the stuff!" said the King. "But what's this?" They looked around and saw that the top of the gas stove was beginning to bend. Suddenly with a Crack! it shot up in the air and the top of the cake appeared, rising slowly.

"Tch, tch!" said the King. "Now, look what you've done! You put in too much yeast!"

The cake went on rising until, at last, it was pressing against the ceiling, which began to crack.

The cook and the King rushed upstairs and when they got to the top they saw the cake had gone right through the ceiling to the floor above.

"Do something, my good man!" shouted the King. The poor cook didn't know what to do. So he jumped up and sat on the cake to stop it rising.

But it went on rising just the same till the cook felt his head bump on the ceiling. A moment later his head went through the roof and still the cake went on rising.

"Oh, Your Majesty! Please go and turn the gas off!" shouted the cook.

The King rushed downstairs and turned the gas off. Then he got his telescope and went into the garden.

The cake had stopped rising, but the top was very high up in the air.

"Oh, drat the man!" said the King. "If he doesn't come down soon there won't be anyone to cook the dinner." Then he thought, "If the cook started to eat the cake, then he would get lower and lower." So he called out, "Cook, eat the cake, at once!"

"Delighted, Your Majesty," called back the cook, and he took a bite. "Yum, yum!" he said. "This is nice cake!"

"Oh, stop talking," said the King, "and eat it up as fast as you can, or I shall have no dinner."

"Right, Your Majesty," said the cook, and ate as fast as he could. But it was such a big cake that it took him two weeks to eat it all and it made him very fat. But the poor King, who was waiting for his dinner, got thinner and thinner.

"Never mind, Your Majesty," called the cook when he had eaten the cake and reached the ground. "I'll cook you a lovely dinner now!" And he did.

So instead of the King being fat and the cook being thin, there was a very thin King and a very fat cook!
Donald Bissett

Discuss the story.

Do the children know any other stories about food? What are their favourites?

Lots of nursery rhymes are food related too: *Little Jack Horner, Little Miss Muffet, Simple Simon, The Queen of Hearts, Sing a Song of Sixpence* . . .

2.50–3.30

ART: POTATO PRINTING

Getting ready

Materials:

Potatoes
Knives and Plates
Paper
Water and brushes
Paint (water colour or poster paint)

1 Cut a potato in two with a sharp knife.
2 Make sure that the cut leaves a very flat surface.
3 Cut the potato again to make the shape that you want to print.

Printing

Method 1

Put the paint on a plate and dilute with a little water (if necessary). Soak the potato block you have made in this colour. Use it like a rubber stamp, pressing the coloured surface onto a piece of paper.

Method 2

Colour the surface of the block with a brush soaked in water colour.
Press the block onto a piece of paper.
Try using your stamp in different ways.

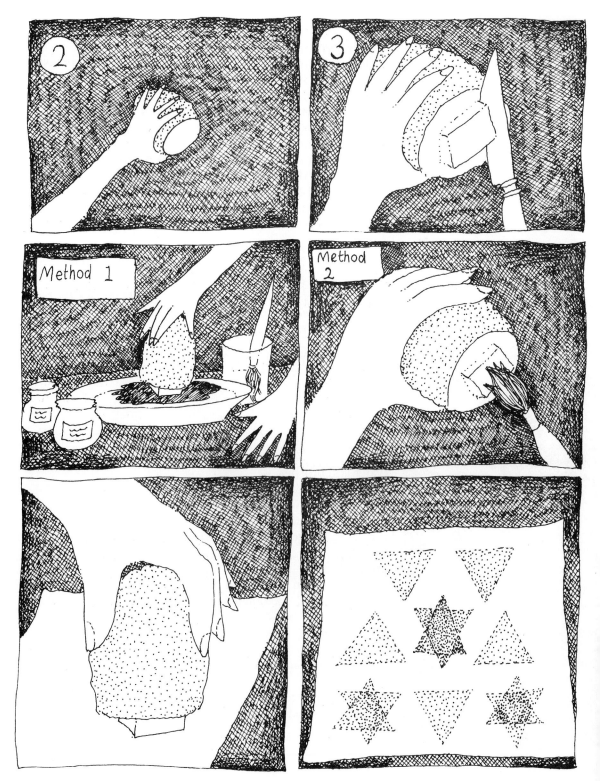

92

Theme: Fair Dinkum Aussies

PREPARATION

1 Write the list of Aussie words on board (see pages 93–4).
2 Make copies of Sheet 26, *Dinkum Aussie Passport.*
3 Write the *Ironbark Bill* passage on board (see pages 94–5).
4 Make copies of Sheet 21, *Test Scoreboard.*
5 Make copies of Sheet 8, *Become an Instant Aussie Author.*
6 Write the poem *Shifting Camp* on board or chart (see page 98).
7 Make copies of Sheet 25, *Positively Ozitively Answer Sheet.*

This might seem like a lot of preparation. We have suggested that you copy the sheets above to save you time, but you could put activities like the *Become an Instant Aussie Author* on a large chart so that you could use it over and over again. Or, if you have access to an overhead projector, you could prepare an overhead transparency sheet. This would reduce the number of sheets you would use in one day. Similarly the *Test Scoreboard* could be written on the board. It just depends on how much time you have.

The sheets we have suggested for today's work are not simply fill-in activities or mindless *busy work.* They demand imaginative effort and much discussion both before and after they are completed.

8.55–9.00	Read the advice given on page 37.
9.00–9.10	Settling in
9.10–9.15	Tell the children that you are going to have an Aussie day. Show them the list of Aussie words you have put on the board. (Select about ten from the list below.) Tell them that they can build on the list by writing their new words on the board whenever they have finished any of their work. Challenge the Grade to get to thirty.

Aussie words

Anzac	mate
billabong	swagman
Woop Woop	whacko
billycan	whinger
Black Stump	spin a yarn
bloke	Eureka
bobby-dazzler	corroboree

brumby	eucalypt
Bunyip	magpie
coo-ee	kookaburra
digger	bushranger
dinkum	damper
Aborigine	witchetty grub
larrikin	jackeroo

9.15–9.45

THE DINKUM AUSSIE PASSPORT
Hand out this Sheet, number 26. The children will not finish by 9.45 so they can keep it and finish off items during the day.

9.45–10.00

SWITCH AROUND
This *Sure Fire Success* (see page 4) will give you a chance to know the children better, and you can try to remember as many of their names as you can. A small plan of names and desks will help.

10.00–10.30

PUNCTUATION SOUND EFFECTS
Discuss these punctuation marks with the children and practise the sound effects for each.

.	full stop — clap hands
,	comma — whistle
;	semi-colon — clap hands and whistle
:	colon — clap hands twice
" **or** "	quotation marks — click tongue twice
!	exclamation mark — ssss and clap hands
?	question mark — click fingers and clap hands
'	apostrophe — click tongue once

Now read the passage below (which you have written on the board), with the children joining in for the punctuation. Introduce the passage by telling the children:

Ironbark Bill was cooking his tea on the banks of the Murrumbidgee river when a bunyip swam up and made a terrifying roar. Ironback Bill took no notice.

Now read on:

"Why didn't you get the wind up?"* asked the bunyip, which was about ten feet long with a body like a Murray Cod with gleaming golden yellow scales, flippers like a crocodile, and the head of an old man. His hair was coarse and long like a horse's mane. "Maybe it's because you've got a cabbage tree hat with methylated spirit corks," went on the bunyip. "When I bellow at the boys from the bush they get the breeze up and run for miles."

94

"I ain't got the breeze up and it ain't nothing to do with me old hat!" said Ironbark.

* this means to get scared

As a variation, give a small piece of dictation. Dictate the punctuation sounds as well as the words, using the sound signals you have established.

(*click click*) I ain(*click*)t a boy from the bush and I ain(*click*)t running for miles (*clap*) I(*click*)ve just boiled me billy and I reckon on drinking it and spending the night here (*clap, click click*)
The bunyip started groaning like a hundred mopokes in a torture chamber (*clap*) Ironbark went on pouring out his tea (*clap*)
(*click click*) Why don(*click*)t you beat it for the scrub (*click fingers and clap hands, click click*) asked the bunyip (*clap*)
(*click click*) Maybe it(*click*)s because you(*click*)ve got a hat (*ssss and clap hands, click click*)

These paragraphs are taken from *Ironbark Bill meets the Bunyip* by Dal Stivens.

10.30–10.45	Recess
10.45–11.30	MATHS: TEST SCOREBOARD
	Discuss this Sheet (number 21) with the children. Give them time to complete it, then correct.
11.30–12.15	STORY

That There Dog of Mine

Macquarie the shearer had met with an accident. To tell the truth, he had been in a drunken row at a wayside shanty, from which he had escaped with three fractured ribs, a cracked head, and various minor abrasions. His dog, Tally, had been a sober but savage participator in the drunken row, and had escaped with a broken leg. Macquarie afterwards shouldered his swag and staggered and struggled along the track ten miles to the Union Town hospital. Lord knows how he did it. He didn't exactly know himself. Tally limped behind all the way, on three legs.

The doctors examined the man's injuries and were surprised at his endurance. Even doctors are surprised

95

sometimes — though they don't always show it. Of course they would take him in, but they objected to Tally. Dogs were not allowed on the premises.

"You will have to turn that dog out," they said to the shearer, as he sat on the edge of a bed.

Macquarie said nothing.

"We cannot allow dogs about the place, my man," said the doctor in a louder tone, thinking the man was deaf.

"Tie him up in the yard then."

"No. He must go out. Dogs are not permitted on the grounds."

Macquarie rose slowly to his feet, shut his agony behind his set teeth, painfully buttoned his shirt over his hairy chest, took up his waistcoat, and staggered to the corner where the swag lay.

"What are you going to do?" they asked.

"You ain't going to let my dog stop?"

"No. It's against the rules. There are no dogs allowed on the premises."

He stooped and lifted his swag, but the pain was too great, and he leaned back against the wall.

"Come, come now! man alive!" exclaimed the doctor, impatiently. "You must be mad. You know you are not in a fit state to go out. Let the wardsman help you to undress."

"No!" said Macquarie. "No. If you won't take my dog in you don't take me. He's got a broken leg and wants fixing up just — just as much as — as I do. If I'm good enough to come in, he's good enough — and — and better."

He paused awhile, breathing painfully, and then went on.

"That — that there old dog of mine has follered me faithful and true, these twelve long hard and hungry years. He's about — about the only thing that ever cared whether I lived or fell and rotted on the cursed track."

He rested again; then he continued:

"That — that there dog was pupped on the track," he said, with a sad sort of a smile. "I carried him for months in a billy, and afterwards on my swag when he knocked up. . . . And the old slut — his mother — she'd foller along quite contented — and sniff the billy now and again — just to see if he was all right. . . . She follered me for God knows how many years. She follered me till she was blind — and for a year after. She follered me till she could crawl along through the dust no longer, and — and then I killed her, because I couldn't leave her behind alive!"

He rested again.

"And this here old dog," he continued, touching Tally's upturned nose with his knotted fingers, "this here old dog has follered me for — for ten years; through floods and droughts, through fair times and — and hard — mostly hard; and kept me from going mad when I had no mate nor money on the lonely track; and watched over me for weeks when I was drunk — drugged and poisoned at the cursed shanties; and saved my life more'n once, and got kicks and curses very often for thanks; and forgave me for it all; and — and fought for me. He was the only living thing that stood up for me against the crawling push of curs when they set onter me at the shanty back yonder — and he left his mark on some of 'em too; and — and so did I."

He took another spell.

Then he drew in his breath, shut his teeth hard, shouldered his swag, stepped into the doorway, and faced round again.

The dog limped out of the corner and looked up anxiously.

"That there dog," said Macquarie to the hospital staff in general, "is a better dog than I'm a man — or you too, it seems — and a better Christian. He's

96

been a better mate to me than I ever was to any man — or any man to me. He's watched over me; kep' me from getting robbed many a time; fought for me; saved my life and took drunken kicks and curses for thanks — and forgave me. He's been a true, straight, honest, and faithful mate to me — and I ain't going to desert him now. I ain't going to kick him out in the road with a broken leg. I — Oh, my God! my back!"

He groaned and lurched forward, but they caught him, slipped off the swag, and laid him on a bed.

Half an hour later the shearer was comfortably fixed up. "Where's my dog?" he asked, when he came to himself.

"Oh, the dog's all right," said the nurse, rather impatiently. "Don't bother. The doctor's setting his leg out in the yard."

Henry Lawson

This story never fails to evoke strong responses from the children.
Discuss it. Talk about Henry Lawson, Banjo Paterson and their stories and poems.
(Have an Australian ballad or two on hand, in case the children are very interested.)
Talk about treatment of pets and Macquarie's feelings towards his dog.

Then ask the children to write a very short story. Give them a small page of lined paper so that no one will be overwhelmed. Topics might include *A sad story, A happy story, An Aussie story, An animal story.*
If there is time, illustrate stories.

Draw your dog here: Friday 13th June

That There Dog of Mine

12.15–12.30	Supervise lunch
12.30–1.15	Lunch break
1.15–1.45	BECOME AN INSTANT AUSSIE AUTHOR This is Sheet 8. Do a couple of stories with the whole class. Then let the children make up their own. Read some of these to the class. The only problem you are likely to encounter with this activity is that once they have laughed their way through three or four different stories the children want to do more and more and more and more and more . . .
1.45–2.05	AUSTRALIAN POEM

Shifting Camp

Glint of gumtrees in the dawn,
so million coloured; bush wind-borne
magpie-music, rising, falling;
and voices of the stockmen calling.

Bellowing of cattle; stamping,
impatient of the place of camping;
bark of dogs; and the crack-crack-crack
of stockwhips as we take the track.

Neighing of night-rested mounts . . .
This is a day that really counts:
a day to ride with a hundred head,
and a roll of canvas — That's my bed.

Rex Ingamells

You may like to read the poem through several times and talk about it. (It helps if the poem is on the board.)
Or you might look at the poem more closely with the children. Consider some of these questions:
  Why is the poem called *Shifting Camp?*
  Do the kind of things described in the poem still happen today?
  What was the scene like at dawn?
  What sounds might you hear?
  Why do you think it might be "this . . . day that really counts"?
  Do you think the stockman would have a comfortable night's sleep?

Talk about the "roll of canvas". Have you ever been camping? What do you sleep on?

2.05–2.15   AUSSIE SONG
Select one that the children know. Preferably have a selection of folk songs on cassette.
Popular choice at Rosevern is *Click Go the Shears*.

2.15–2.30   Recess

2.30–2.40   SKETCH AUSTRALIA
Hand everyone a sheet of paper. Name on top. Then give the instruction: draw a map of Australia without copying from an atlas, wall chart or exercise book.
   This is a delightful activity. Pin the sketches on a notice board. Whose is the most correct? Whose is the funniest? Whose is even better than the shape we're in?

2.40–3.10   POSITIVELY OZITIVELY ANSWER SHEET
This is Sheet 25.
After sheets have been distributed, ask the children if they have any problems or queries. You may need to explain some of the *What are? Who Are?* questions.

3.10–3.30   Since you won't have time to do all these, choose the activities which are more important to you.

Quickly correct (as a class) the *Positively Ozitively Answer Sheet*.
Collect *Passports* and discuss (if time).
Ask the children for permission to take the Passports home. (This will help if you have the class again, later in the year.)
Look at the Aussie word list. How many more have the fast finishers added? Can you think of more?
Finish off with an *Aussie song* again.

or
Give a prize — 2 witchetty grubs — for anyone in the grade who can sing or speak the first two lines of *Advance Australia Fair*.

Themeless Theme

PREPARATION

1 Make copies of Sheet 7, *The Big Rock Candy Mountains*.
2 Prepare on board *The Ancient Egyptian Multiplication Method* (see pages 101–3).
3 Get a bundle of picture story books from the library (see page 32).
4 Bat, ball and wicket for continuous cricket.
5 Prepare the *Cloud Chart* (see page 106).

8.55–9.00

Before you do ANYTHING, it is essential to read the advice given on page 37. For your own sanity — particularly with a Grade 6 — it is well worth the few minutes spent.

We have prepared two days for Grade 6 — one, a theme day (*Mystery*) and this one, a more formal day. If you prepare well, things will run more smoothly.

9.00–9.45

FOR STARTERS: WRITE A STORY
Retell a traditional story.

The children can tell the story straight, or give an up-tempo funny version. At Rosevern we have given them *The Three Bears*, *The Three Pigs*, and *Little Red Riding Hood*, and they never fail.

The insecure writers all know the stories and can get them right; the good writers can exercise their wit and imagination with variety and humour.

Give them a single sheet of paper each so that the task is not daunting for them or for you. Assure them that you will read all their stories. Fast finishers will probably write more than a page, after which they can design and illustrate.

Display all stories when they are completed. (If possible reserve a space on the display board and staple the heading GRADE 6 STORIES.)

9.45–10.00

MATHS: QUICK PROBLEMS
Automatic response is as much a listening comprehension activity as it is maths. You will be surprised how often the children ask you to repeat the problems.

1 How many hours in 660 minutes?	*11 hours*
2 Write half past two in a shorter way.	*2.30*
3 $7 \times 9 = \ldots$	*63*
4 How many feet on the three blind mice?	*12*
5 $8 \times 4 + 15 = \ldots$	*47*
6 Days in June, July and August?	*92*

7 $1\frac{1}{2} + 2$ quarters = ...   2

8 Sydney is 800 kilometres from your home town. How far
  would it be to travel from home to Sydney and back,
  twice?   *3200 km*

9 Millimetres in 3 cm?   *30 mm*

10 $3 \times 13 = ...$ *39*

11 Metres in $2\frac{1}{2}$ kilometres?   *2500 m*

12 $29 - 8 = ...$ *21*

13 Kilograms in $2\frac{1}{2}$ tonnes?   *2500 kg*

14 How many years since you were born?   *Check.*

15 $1\frac{1}{4}$ centuries. How many years?   *125*

16 Your height in centimetres, approximately.   *Check.*

17 You haven't slept for three days and nights in a row. How
   long have you remained awake?   *72 hours*

18 Estimate the number of heart beats in a minute.   *Check.*

19 $48 \div 2 = ...$ *24*

20 Half a litre. How many millilitres?   *500 ml*

21 $23 + 24 - 23 - 24 = ...$ *0*

22 How much is 5 kilo of potatoes @ 70c a kilo?   *$3.50*

23 Which is heavier: a kilo of cotton wool or a kilo of
   stones?   *Same*

24 Number of years a child spends at school if she starts in the
   Prep year and finishes at Year 11?   *12*

25 $48 - 19 = ...$ *29*

26 $13 \times 12 = ...$ *156*

27 Double, double 4 = ...   *16*

28 5 Christmas cards @ 95 c = ...   *$4.75*

29 Sides in a cube?   *6*

30 15 equations right out of 30. What percentage correct?   *50%*

Correct problems. Was anyone 100% right?

10.00–10.30

FUNNY COMPREHENSION: THE BIG ROCK CANDY
MOUNTAINS
This is Sheet 7.
Children answer questions in sentences in their language
books. Make sure you collect the sheets after the lesson, so that
you can use them again.

10.30–10.45

Recess

10.45–11.30

MATHS: THE ANCIENT EGYPTIAN MULTIPLICATION METHOD
First revise a few short multiplication equations.

24	168	472	1674
× 6	× 5	× 3	× 9

This will increase children's confidence. Correct and discuss.
Ask about long multiplication. How many know how to do it?
Do the refined version on the board:

$$
\begin{array}{r}
34 \\
\times\ 21 \\
\hline
34 \\
680 \\
\hline
714
\end{array}
$$

Now tell them that you are going to show them a different way
— the Ancient Egyptian way.

1 Numbers in the left-hand column are doubled.

2 Those in the right-hand column are halved and any remainder is left out.

$$
\begin{array}{r}
34 \times 21 \\
68 \times 10 \\
136 \times\ \ 5 \\
272 \times\ \ 2 \\
544 \times\ \ 1 \\
\hline
714 \\
\hline
\end{array}
$$

3 When the numbers in the right hand column are even the whole row is crossed out.

4 To find the answer, the numbers remaining in the left hand column are added together and HEY PRESTO! — the answer.

Here are some other examples. Put just the first lines on the board and let the children work them out. We've printed the whole process here just on the off chance that you make a mistake!

102

1	24 × 14	2	16 × 19	3	18 × 22
	48 × 7		32 × 9		36 × 11
	96 × 3		64 × 4		72 × 5
	192 × 1		128 × 2		144 × 2
			256 × 1		288 × 1
	336		304		396

4 If 64 Egyptians carted 12 rocks a day to the pyramids, how many stones would get there in a week?
First find out many rocks carted in a day.

64 × 12	Then, to find how many stones are	768 × 7
128 × 6	carted in a week, multiply the	1536 × 3
256 × 3	answer by 7.	3072 × 1
512 × 1		
		5376
768		

STORY — DISCUSSION — WRITING

J. Roodie

J. Roodie was wild and bad, although he was only nine. Nobody owned him, so he lived in a creek bed with his animals, who had nasty names. His dog was called Grip, which was what it did to passers-by. He had a bad-tempered brumby called Kick, and a raggedy crow called Pincher. Pincher swooped down and stole kids' twenty cents worth of chips when they came out of the fish and chip shop. J. Roodie had trained him to do that.

Nobody ever went for a stroll along the creek, because they knew better. J. Roodie kept a supply of dried cow manure and used it as ammunition, because he didn't have pleasant manners at all. He never had a bath and his fingernails were a disgrace and a shame.

There was a cottage near the creek with a FOR SALE notice, but no one wanted to live near J. Roodie. Everyone muttered, 'Someone should do something about that awful J. Roodie!' but nobody knew what to do and they were too scared to get close enough to do it, anyhow.

J. Roodie painted creek mud scars across his face, and blacked out his front teeth. He drew biro tattoos over his back and he stuck a metal ring with a piece missing through his nose so that it looked pierced. He swaggered around town and pulled faces at babies in prams and made them bawl, and he filled the kindergarten sandpit with quicksand. Luckily the teacher discovered it before she lost any pupils.

He let Grip scare everyone they met, and he let Kick eat people's prize roses, and he was just as much a nuisance going out of town as he was going in. But nobody came and told him off, because they were all nervous of tough J. Roodie and his wild animals.

One day he was annoyed to see that the FOR SALE notice had been removed from the cottage and someone had moved in. He sent Grip over to scare them away.

Grip bared his fangs and slobbered like a hungry wolf at the little old lady who had just moved in.

'Oh, what a sweet puppy!' said the little old lady whose name was Miss Daisy Thrimble. Grip had never been called 'sweet' before, so he stopped slobbering and wagged his tail. Miss Daisy Thrimble gave him a bath and fluffed up his coat with a hair dryer. 'I'll call you Curly,' she said. 'Here's a nice mat for you, Curly.'

Grip felt self-conscious about going back to J. Roodie with his coat all in little ringlets, and besides, the mat was cosier than a creek bed, so he went to sleep.

J. Roodie waited two days for him and then he sent Pincher to the cottage. Miss Daisy was hanging out washing. 'Caaaaawwrk!' Pincher croaked horribly, flapping his big, raggedy, untidy wings and snapping his beak.

'What a poor little lost bird,' said Miss Daisy. She plucked Pincher out of the sky and carried him inside. She filled a saucer with canary seed and fetched a mirror and a bell. 'I'll call you Pretty Boy,' she said. 'And I'll teach you how to talk.'

Pincher already knew some not very nice words that J. Roodie taught him, but Miss Daisy Thrimble looked so sweet-faced and well-behaved that Pincher didn't say them. He tapped the bell with his beak, and looked in the little mirror, and decided that it was very nice to have playthings.

J. Roodie grew tired of waiting for Pincher, and he sent Kick to scare Miss Daisy away. Kick pawed the lawn and carried on like a rodeo and rolled his eyes till the whites showed.

'Oh, what a darling little Shetland pony!' said Miss Daisy. She caught Kick and brushed away the creek mud and plaited his mane into rosettes tied up with red ribbons. 'There's a cart in the shed,' she said. 'You can help me do the shopping. I'll call you Twinkle.'

Kick snorted indignantly, but then he saw his reflection in a kitchen window and was amazed that he could look so dignified. He stopped worrying about his new name when Miss Daisy brought him a handful of oats.

J. Roodie marched over to the cottage and yelled, 'YAAAAH!' at the top of his voice. He jumped up and down and brandished a spear and rattled some coconuts with faces painted on them, which were tied to his belt. They looked just like shrunken heads. 'WHEEEEEE!' yelled J. Roodie. 'GRRRRRRR!'

'What a dear little high-spirited boy!' said Miss Daisy. 'But you certainly need a bath.' She dumped J. Roodie into a tub and when she had finished scrubbing, he was as clean and sweet-smelling as an orange. Miss Daisy dressed him in a blue checked shirt and nice clean pants and brushed his hair. 'There,' she said. 'I shall call you Joe. I'll be proud to take you into town with me in my little cart.'

She sat Joe Roodie next to her, and

Kick, called Twinkle now, trotted smartly into town, and Grip, called Curly now, ran beside and didn't nip anyone they met.

People said. 'Good morning, Miss Daisy. Is that your little nephew?'

'His name is Joe,' Miss Daisy said proudly. 'I think he lived in the creek bed before he came to stay with me.'

'He can't have,' they said. 'J. Roodie lives in the creek bed and he'd never let anyone else live there.'

'J. who?' asked Miss Daisy, because she was rather hard of hearing. 'Do you know anyone called J. something or other, Joe?'

Joe Roodie didn't answer right away. He'd just felt in the pockets of his new pants and found a pocket knife with six blades, and a ball of red twine, and some interesting rusty keys, and eleven marbles.

'We'll buy some apples and make a pie for our supper,' said Miss Daisy. 'Maybe we could invite that J. boy they said lives in the creek. What do you think, Joe?'

Joe Roodie hadn't tasted apple pie for as many years as he hadn't had a bath, and his mouth watered.

'There used to be a kid called J. Roodie in the creek bed,' he said. 'But he doesn't live there anymore.'

Robin Klein

Discuss the story and Robin Klein's other books.

Then play the game **That's Good/That's Bad**. (Remember: J. Roodie changed from being wild and bad, to being good.) This can be done orally on the board

OR

As a written exercise

OR

Children work in pairs, one making a statement, and the other replying either *That's good* or *That's bad*. The storyline changes as it goes along.

Here is an example:

Child 1: A man went for a trip in an aeroplane.
Child 2: Oh, that's good.
Child 1: No, it's bad — the plane had a faulty motor.
Child 2: Oh, that's bad.
Child 1: No, it's good — he had a parachute.
Child 2: Oh, that's good.
Child 1: No, it's bad — the parachute collapsed.
Child 2: Oh, that's bad.
Child 1: No, it's good — he landed in a haystack.
Child 2: That's good.
Child 1: No, it's bad — there was a pitchfork in the haystack!

Other titles could be:
A man went to have a haircut ...
A lady went for a swim ...
A girl went to a supermarket ...
Two 6th graders stayed away from school ...
A boy went to the dentist ...
It was Mum's birthday ...

12.15–12.30	Supervise lunch
12.30–1.15	Lunch break
1.15–1.40	U.S.S.R.: QUIET READING TIME

Read this activity as described on page 32.

We are not including this activity as teacher's rest time: it DOES work, and it DOES keep the children quiet; and straight after lunch is often a time when Grade 6's need settling down.

If you decide to use picture books, you may talk to the children about the value of these books, and how lots of titles are far more suitable for adults and older children than for younger children. E.g. *Patatrac* — J. Loup (Cape); The *Asterix* series — Goscinny & Uderzo (Hodder); *The Shrinking of Treehorn* — F. P. Heide (Puffin); *Fungus the Bogeyman* — R. Briggs (Hamish Hamilton); *Sir Gawain and the Loathly Damsel* — J. Troughton (Puffin).

1.40–2.15   PHYSICAL EDUCATION: CONTINUOUS CRICKET

Continuous cricket is always popular and is enjoyed equally by boys and girls. Everyone knows the rules and therefore there are fewer arguments, nor do you have to explain the rules before you start.

There are variations of continuous cricket but basically it resembles the game *Kickball* (a *Sure Fire Success*: see page 17). Instead of using a large rubber ball and kicking, use a rounders or cricket bat, and a smaller ball, e.g. a tennis ball.

You may need to place a limit on the number of runs any one individual can score before retiring. Also organise a scorer for each team to prevent arguments.

2.15–2.30   Recess

2.30–3.30   SCIENCE AND ART: CLOUDS

Draw on board the common types of clouds:

cirrus   **cumulus**   **stratus**   **nimbus**

Discuss different types of clouds — when they occur and why. Which ones indicate rain? — e.g. rain falls from low clouds such as nimbostratus or cumulonimbus. Cirrus clouds give us the first indication that rain is on the way. (Books on Clouds and Weather are found in the 551 section of the Dewey Decimal Classification System in your school or local library.)

Go outside to look at the clouds, and sketch them. A note-pad or jotter and ordinary soft pencil are best.

Then you could choose one of these options:

Discussion

The kinds of clouds you can see today.

Our forecasts.

Describe a cloud to someone who is blind.

Have you ever been in an aeroplane among the clouds? How do clouds look? What do you think they would feel like? Imagine if you could step out of the plane and lie on the clouds. (Don't try it please!)

Clouds and fog — the differences.

Look at your sketch. Does it remind you of anything? Make one of your sketches into a picture.

Project work

The children present their findings about clouds in their science books. Divide the page into sections. Draw clouds and make headings. Do a little research on the different kinds of clouds.

Note

The success of the activities on clouds is dependent on some co-operation from children in the grade, particularly if they are to go outside the classroom at various times.

If the grade is riotous, simply abandon the cloud activities, ask them to get out their spelling books, rule up and begin:

ONE HUNDRED SPELLING DEMONS

which	can't	guess	they	used	answer	grammar	piece
their	sure	says	half	always	two	minute	raise
there	loose	having	break	where	too	any	ache
separate	lose	just	buy	women	ready	much	read
don't	Wednesday	doctor	again	done	forty	beginning	said
meant	country	whether	very	hear	hour	blue	hoarse
business	February	believe	none	here	trouble	though	shoes
many	know	knew	week	write	among	coming	tonight
friend	could	laid	often	writing	busy	early	wrote
some	seems	tear	whole	heard	built	instead	thought
been	Tuesday	choose	won't	does	eighty	easy	sugar
since	wear	tired	cough	once	making	through	straight
				would	dear	every	truly

GRADE 6 DAY TWO

Theme: Mystery

This is the second of two days for Grade 6. A *Mystery Day* will be great fun, especially if you can spare some time at home and before school in preparing the games and sheets — either on the board, on duplicated sheets, on charts or wall-hangings. If you prepare well, it will help to create the mysterious atmosphere for the day, and will make things run smoothly. Take a few minutes NOW to read the advice on page 37.

PREPARATION

1 Write on board (and cover up) the mysterious spelling words (see below).
2 Write Egyptian hieroglyphic numerals on board or chart (see page 109).
3 Make copies of Sheet 30, *Is It a Flying Saucer . . . Is It a Donut?*, or make a chart using the ideas.
4 Make copies of Sheet 20, *Mysterious Treasure Hunt*.
5 Prepare 10 cm squares of white card, and draw the colour coded circle on the board, for the *Seemingly Magic Colour Disc* (see pages 111–2).
6 Make a simple black ghost (see page 116).

8.58–9.00

Write on the board: *How many smaller words can you make from MYSTERIOUS?* This is for the fast-finishers who whine, "I've finished — what will I do now?"
The record so far is 145 words, but few children would be able to get even half that number. Forty should be a posssibility.

9.01–9.05

Bring the class in and sort out administration, etc.

9.05–9.35

SPELLING
A formal start, but the words are exciting and mysterious words. Speak clearly and firmly. Say the word first, use it in a sentence, then repeat the word. Allow the children enough time to write the words carefully in their books. Add any other words you can think of, and delete any you dislike.

dreaming	thoughts	errie	EEEEEK! (a	Open Sesame!
voo doo	abracadabra	werewolves	tricky one)	wand
spirits	vampires	jinx	superstition	spells
U F O	mystery	hoo doo	flying saucers	corroboree
genie	E S P	Nargun	miracle	life
enchanted	uncanny	magic circle	curses	Heaven
wishes			Dreamtime	

Now read the list of words, so that children can check over their own lists. Then spell the words out, slowly and clearly. Children correct their own work. Uncover the words, which you have written on the board (hide them behind a map or chart). This will enable all children to double-check their work. With E S P and U F O say *Capital E, Capital S, Capital P* or, if you are clever, *Extra Sensory Perception.* Do the same with U F O — Unidentified Flying Object. EEEEEK! must have exactly five E's. Ask: "Hands up those who got 31 correct?" and express dismay at the result. Go through 30, 29, 28, 27, 26, 25 . . .

Then ask the class to look again at words they spelt incorrectly. Use the Cripps' technique of LOOK, COVER, WRITE and CHECK. See page 60.

9.35—9.45

DISCUSSION

Children are fascinated by the occult and by mysterious events. They will probably be eager to discuss these topics. If they are settled, this should be encouraged. If, however, they are over-responsive and noisy, cut the discussion and go on with the next activity.

9.45—10.10

CRACK THE CODE: HIEROGLYPHICS

Children love Egyptian hieroglyphics. They are ancient and mysterious, yet at the same time easy to draw and work out. As well, there is the distinct advantage for the teacher in that they are simple to draw on the chalkboard or charts.

Before asking the children to solve the Ancient Egyptian Mathematical Mysteries, tell them a little about hieroglyphics: The word *hieroglyphics* means *priestly writing.* The Greeks gave it this name because they thought that only Egyptian priests could use the code.

Hieroglyphics is a kind of picture writing made up of images of people, animals, birds, plants and everyday things.

The Ancient Egyptians used hieroglyphics to represent numbers as well as words. They did not write numbers as units, tens, hundreds, and so on: they just added symbols side by side to get the number.

Tell the children to copy these hieroglyphic numbers into their books:

Stroke	Arch	Coiled rope	Lotus flower	Pointed finger	Tadpole	Astonished man
I	∩	?	⚶	⟋	⬭	⚿
1	10	100	1 000	10 000	100 000	1 000 000

Then ask them to write some numbers in hieroglyphics.

223 = 𝟡 𝟡∩∩|||

1141 = 𐤀 𝟡∩∩∩∩|

9 = |||(|||||

112 121 = ◇ ↗ 𐤀𐤀 𝟡∩∩|

Can they solve these equations using the hieroglyphic code?

1 𐤀𝟡∩∩ **plus** 𐤀𐤀 **equals** . . . . .

2 ∩∩∩∩∩||||||| **plus** 𝟡𝟡 **equals** . . . . .

3 𝟡∩∩∩ | **plus** 𝟡∩∩∩∩ **equals** . . . . .

4 𐤀𝟡𝟡 **minus** ∩∩|||| **equals** . . . . .

5 ∩∩∩∩|| **plus** 𝟡∩| **plus** 𝟡𐤀𝟡𝟡∩| **equals** . . . . .

For the fast finishers: write Egyptian numerals for your age, this year, the year you were born.
(Really fast finishers could have a go at the *Porta Alphabet Code* — see Sheet 27, or the *Ancient Egyptian Multiplication Method* — see pages 101–103.)

10.10–10.30

"IS IT A FLYING SAUCER . . . . .?"
Use Sheet 30, or a large chart with the pictures on it. Look at the first picture and talk about the title. "Is it a flying saucer, is it a donut? — no, it's a Mexican seen from above!" The children soon get the idea. Then they use their jotters to supply titles for all the other pictures.
When most of them have finished naming the pictures, encourage them to swap titles. They'll enjoy each other's efforts almost as much as their own.
If there is time before recess, let the children work in groups or pairs to make up their own pictures and see if the others can guess the title. Share with the grade. Display as many as you can (with titles). You will find it difficult to stop them from pursuing this activity. Believe it or not, many of ours stayed in over recess, producing more and more pictures.

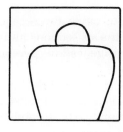 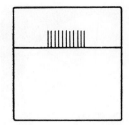

Grandfather in armchair   **Eleven soldiers presenting arms, or is it Billy's new hairstyle?**

10.30–10.45	Recess

10.45–11.30 MAGICAL, MYSTICAL MATHS

Part 1: Birthday magic

Begin by saying: I have a special formula which enables me to tell your birthday.

1 Write the number for the month you were born. (January = 1, December = 12)
2 Multiply this by 5.
3 Add 6.
4 Multiply by 4.
5 Add 9.
6 Multiply by 5.
7 Add the date you were born.
8 Subtract 165 from the total.

The last two numbers tell the date you were born; the first number or numbers will be the month you were born.

Magic?

Try it with your friends' birthdays.

Part 2: Mysterious treasure hunt

This is Sheet 20. Children write their answers on the stepping stones, or on a separate sheet of paper if you want to keep the sheets for another day.

11.30–12.15 SCIENCE: THE SEEMINGLY MAGIC COLOUR DISC

Cut squares of white card approximately 10 cm × 10 cm. Distribute one between two children.

Show the children how to make a magic colour disc.

1 Draw a circle, using compasses or something to trace around.

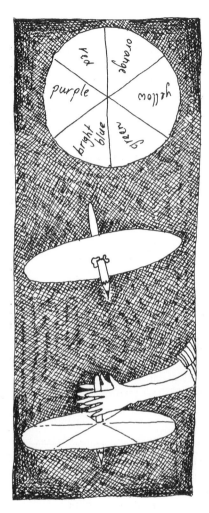

2 Divide the circle into six equal parts.
3 Colour the six sections in this order:
red, orange, yellow, green, blue and
purple.
The last three colours of the rainbow
are: blue, indigo and violet, but for this
experiment we have combined indigo
(dark blue) and violet — and called it
purple.
4 Make a hole in the middle of the circle
and attach a pencil with tape or Blu-tack.
5 Spin the disc as fast as possible

Any colours can be made by mixing the three primary colours
— yellow, red and blue. In theory you can even make black by
mixing these three colours, but in practice it doesn't really work
because you must have pure paint. The closest you will get with
ordinary paints is a murky-looking dark brown.

The only colour you cannot get is white. It seems to have no
colour, but it actually contains them all. If you split up white
light by looking at it through raindrops or a piece of cut glass,
you wil see all the colours of the rainbow. That is why, if you
can spin your disc fast enough, thus putting all the colours
together again, you will see that it looks white. At first, ours
looked pale green, but when we spun it faster, and made sure
that the disc was fastened securely underneath with blutack or
sticky tape, it actually turned white! We were excited to find
that the experiment had really worked.

12.15–12.30	Supervise lunch
12.30–1.15	Lunch break
1.15–1.45	LISTENING AND COMPREHENSION

A quiet activity straight after lunch is usually a sound idea. Read
this piece to the children and ask them to listen intently.

Dead men don't walk — or do they?

On the small island of Haiti many people believe that
magic men can bring dead people back to life and turn
them into slaves. These slaves are known as zombies.

They never close their eyes, or eat much; nor can they talk or think, but they are able to obey commands and to work.

Before the men who are to become zombies die, the magic men walk backwards to their houses. They pull the victims' souls out through a crack in the door and place them in a jar or bottle. Soon the victims become ill and die.

When their families have left them in their graves, the magic men return. They dig them up and let them sniff at their souls. They keep whispering the dead men's names. The dead men then open their eyes and follow blindly.

From then on they become zombies.

Many people have different theories and opinions about zombies. Some think that a live victim is kept like a zombie by secret drugs. So far, no one has discovered drugs which work in this way.

The magic men of Haiti are the only ones who know the truth.

After reading the piece, tell the children that you are going to ask them some questions, so they must listen VERY carefully as you read it a second time. Discuss zombies with the class, then ask some relevant questions.

This could be an oral or written exercise. If you decide to make it written work, read the questions and allow a certain time for them to answer each one.

Your children might find some of these questions difficult. Judging by their oral discussion, you should be able to determine which ones your group will be able to manage.

Name three things which zombies cannot do, and two things they can.

Do we have any "magic men" in our society who have the power to change people's lives and deaths?

What do the magic men do to their victims' souls? Do you think this is possible?

Do you agree that drugs might be used? How would these drugs work?

Do you think that zombies are living people, kept in a drugged condition?

Why do you think the magic men walk backwards to their victims' houses? (There could be many answers to this question.)

Is there a similarity in the deaths of zombies and Australian Aborigines when the bone is pointed at them?

113

U.S.S.R.:   OR AN EERIE POEM
Now would be a good time for quiet reading (*U.S.S.R.* see page 32), but if you want to keep the magic pot boiling, read this poem and then try some eerie, quiet verse speaking.
Read the poem in a hushed, fearful voice.

The Bunyip

Oh, came you up by the place of dread
(West red and the moon low down)
Where no winds blow and the birds have fled
And the gum stands dead and its arms gleam white,
And the tribe sneak by with a stealthy tread
In the ghostly light, in the ghostly light.
Brave Worralong went one grey nightfall
(Awoi! woi!) where the grim rocks frown;
He came no more to the camps at all
(Skies dark, and the moon low down).

As we came up by the gully side
(Deep dusk, and the moon low down)
A dingo whined and a curlew cried
And the reeds replied in hushed affright
Where tall brave Worralong screamed and died
In the ghostly light, in the ghostly light.
For the Thing lurks there in the haunted place
(Awoi! woi!) where the pool is brown,
Where lost ones vanish and leave no trace
(Day dead, and the moon low down).

Oh, go not by near the Bunyip's lair
(Stars dim, and the moon low down)
Or tip-toe past and beware, beware
The dark pool snare and be set for flight,
For things of terror have happened there
In the ghostly light, in the ghostly light.
And in the gunyas we crouch and hark
(Awoi! woi!) where the dead men drown
The monster's bellow across the dark
(Stars gone and the moon low down).

James Devaney

Discussion
Ask several children to tell in their own words what happened
— that is, what is the story of the poem?

Explain that the Australian Aborigines never hit or smack their children. Sometimes they stand the child beside a tree and the parent whacks the tree with such ferocious intensity that the child cries pitifully.

Also, they threaten their children with stories of dreadful creatures that will eat them up if they go anywhere near dangerous waterholes or other forbidden places.

Verse speaking hints

After *you* have read the poem, ask the children to help. In very low voices they say with you the second and last lines of the verses:

In verse I:

  (West red and the moon low down)

  (Skies dark, and the moon low down).

In Verse 2:

  (Deep dusk, and the moon low down)

  (Day dead, and the moon low down).

In Verse 3:

  (Stars dim, and the moon low down)

  (Stars gone and the moon low down).

In each verse they whisper with you, line six:

  In the ghostly light, in the ghostly light,

For the words *Awoi! woi!,* they make a wind-wailing sound. Practise several times.

2.15–2.30	Recess
2.30–3.10	DREAMS

A few facts

Dreams are vague and often confused. Everyone dreams every night. Sometimes we cannot remember our dreams at all, but at other times we can recall them vividly. They are important because they can show us things lying deep in our thoughts, which we have hidden, even from ourselves. Artists have always painted dreams. A group who called themselves *surrealists* tried to paint pictures which had the same feelings in them as dreams. Surrealism means roughly "beyond the things we know in everyday life".

Discussion

After this, discuss with the children their own dreams and nightmares.

They then draw a dream, and write something about it — a description, a poem, a story or a song.

115

3.10–3.30

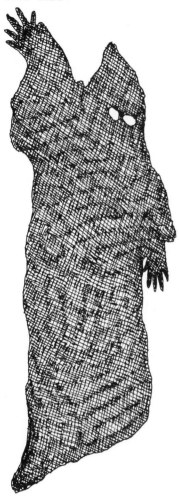

IT'S MAGIC!
Some light-hearted games to conclude the day.
See a ghost
We didn't believe this, but it happens!
Cut out a large simple ghost picture like this from a sheet of black paper.
Stick it onto a white sheet of paper.
Children stare at it without blinking for one full minute.
Then take the ghost picture away, and look at a white or pale wall or board or (ideally) a white projection screen. The image of the ghost materialises before your very eyes!

E S P
Choose a child to leave the room.
Class members decide on a colour, or a number between one and twelve, or a footy team.
The whole class then concentrates violently projecting coloured vibes towards the guesser when he returns to the room.
He is told "We are all thinking of a colour. What is it?"
Now and then a child will fluke an answer. Such a miraculous event will be greeted by incredulous gasps, or cries of "It works! It works!"
Of course, if it doesn't work, all you say is, "Come on try harder. You aren't trying or concentrating hard enough!"

4 Sheets

Forty
Reproducible
Activity Pages

Starting Sounds

Little Red Riding Hood   **SHEET 2**

Once upon a time there lived _____ little girl who had a red

_____ . Her name was Little Red Riding _____ . One day her

mother asked her _____ take a basket of food to _____

grandmother who lived all by herself _____ a tiny house right in the

_____ of a forest.

Before she left, _____ mother said to her, "You must _____ talk

to the wicked wolf who _____ in the forest." On the way, _____

Red Riding Hood saw some pretty _____ . She put the basket down and

_____ to pick them. Suddenly the wicked _____ jumped out and

said, "Where are _____ going, Little Red Riding Hood?" "I'm

_____ to visit my grandmother, who lives _____ a tiny house right

in the _____ of the forest." Then she ran _____ but the wicked

wolf ran straight _____ grandmother's house and got there a

_____ time before Little Red Riding Hood.

Find the Mistakes

The Three Wishes   **SHEET 4**

Once upon a time there lived _____ poor old woodcutter. He lived in _____ house with his wife.

One day _____ was about to cut down a _____ tree when an elf appeared.

"Please _____ cut down this tree," asked the _____ . "I live here. I will give _____ three wishes if you go away."

_____ the woodcutter left.

"Wife, wife, I _____ a surprise. An elf said I _____ have three wishes."

"Fiddle-sticks," said his _____ . "Go back to work at once. _____ a long time since we had _____ food to eat. I'm so hungry _____ wish we could have a huge _____ of sausages."

A huge bowl of _____ appeared on the table. "Help! Where _____ they come from?" said the wife.

"_____ one of the wishes. Let's thank _____ elf," said the woodcutter.

"Fiddle-sticks," said _____ wife. "What a silly wish. Sausage! _____ could have wished for a new _____ , food and wine. But now we _____ a silly bowl of sausages. I _____ the sausages were on the end _____ your nose."

When I Was Very Young

Write about yourself when you were very small. What are your first memories?

122

The Surprise Birthday Party

Find the mistakes.

One evening, on the 25th February, just before breakfast, nine-year-old James Robertson woke up, raced out of bed and rushed to the kitchen. "Mum!" he called, "remember it's my birthday in six days time: on the 30th February!"

"I haven't forgotten," said his Mum, "we're having a surprise birthday party for you. We've invited nine friends — five girls and six boys — Peter, Paul, Mark, Simon, Anthony, Ted, Ivan, Ann, Sarah, Dimetra, Maria, Felicity and Julie."

James couldn't wait for the days to go by. Slowly they passed, until finally it was the 30th February.

The sun shone brightly from an overcast sky, while the rain crashed down, hour after hour.

"What a perfect day for a party," thought Bill Robertson. "The barbecue will be great and I wonder what presents I'll get?"

All ten children arrived early, some time after the party had begun. Everyone brought presents except Russell, who promised to get Bill something soon — before the 24th February.

Bill received a soft pink teddy bear made from wood, a model vintage car — a 1985 Nissan Bluebird, a book: *Charlotte's Web* by E. B. Black, some blue modelling clay to make grass, bushes and trees for the scenery surrounding his electric train set, a record for his cassette player, and several other interesting gifts.

The children played the usual party games: pin the donkey on the tail, widdly tinks, hide and speak, but best of all was the food — party pies, chips, toast and thousands and millions, frunkfarts, but no icecream or lollies.

James blew out the eleven candles and as he cut the birthday cake with a fork, he made a wish, "I wish for another surprise party next year when I will be eleven years old, on the 31st February."

The Big Rock Candy Mountains   SHEET 7

One evening when the sun was low
And the jungle fires were burning,
Down the track came a hobo hamming
And he said: Boys, I'm not turning;
I'm headed for a land that's far away
Beside the crystal fountains.
So come with me, we'll go and see
The Big Rock Candy Mountains.

In the Big Rock Candy Mountains
There's a land that's fair and bright,
Where the handouts grow on bushes
And you sleep out every night,
Where the box-cars all are empty
And the sun shines everyday
On the birds and the bees
And the cigarette trees,
The rock-and-rye springs
Where the whangdoodle sings,
In the Big Rock Candy Mountains.

In the Big Rock Candy Mountains
All the cops have wooden legs
And the bulldogs all have rubber teeth
And the hens lay hard-boiled eggs;
The farmers' trees are full of fruit
And the barns are full of hay:
O I'm bound to go
Where there ain't no snow,
And the rain don't fall,
The wind don't blow,
In the Big Rock Candy Mountains.

In the Big Rock Candy Mountains
You never change your socks
And the little streams of alcohol
Come a-trickling down the rocks:
The shacks all have to tip their hats
And the railroad bulls are blind;
There's a lake of stew,
And of whisky too,
You can paddle all around
In a big canoe,
In the Big Rock Candy Mountains.

In the Big Rock Candy Mountains
The jails are made of tin
And you can bust right out again
As soon as they put you in;
There ain't no short-handled shovels,
No axes, saws or picks:
O I'm going to stay
Where you sleep all day,
Where they hung the Turk
That invented work,
In the Big Rock Candy Mountains.
I'll see you all
This coming fall
In the Big Rock Candy Mountains.

Traditional

1 Why can you get out of jail so quickly in
   the Big Rock Candy Mountains?
2 Why doesn't it hurt when the bulldogs bite you?
3 Is the weather summery or wintery in the Big
   Rock Candy Mountains? How do you know?
4 Why wouldn't you be frightened of policemen?
5 Why do you stagger a bit when you drink
   from the streams or creeks?
6 Would you be likely to have a job as a
   builder, digger (of holes) or a labourer? Why?
7 Would your mother be pleased with the
   freshness of your socks? Why? Why not?
8 How long would it take to cook a
   hard-boiled egg? How do you know?
9 How windy is it?
10 What kind of houses do you sleep in?
11 Where do you buy cigarettes?
12 What sort of a creature is a
    whangdoodle? Describe where it lives,
    what it eats, and what its young are like.
    (You will have to make up all of this.)
13 Is this an unlucky poem?
14 Who invented work, and what happened to him?
15 If you had friends for dinner and you wished
    to serve stew and whisky, what would you do?
16 Would you like to visit The Big Rock
    Candy Mountains? Why?
17 Is this a *true* poem?

Become an Instant Aussie Author   SHEET 8

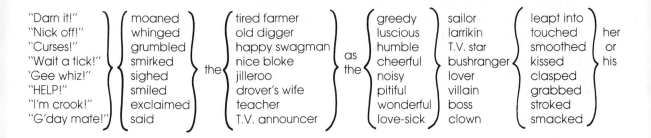

"Darn it!"
"Nick off!"
"Curses!"
"Wait a tick!"
'Gee whiz!'
"HELP!"
"I'm crook!"
"G'day mate!"
} {
moaned
whinged
grumbled
smirked
sighed
smiled
exclaimed
said
}
the
{
tired farmer
old digger
happy swagman
nice bloke
jilleroo
drover's wife
teacher
T.V. announcer
}
as
the
{
greedy
luscious
humble
cheerful
noisy
pitiful
wonderful
love-sick
}
{
sailor
larrikin
T.V. star
bushranger
lover
villain
boss
clown
}
{
leapt into
touched
smoothed
kissed
clasped
grabbed
stroked
smacked
}
her
or
his

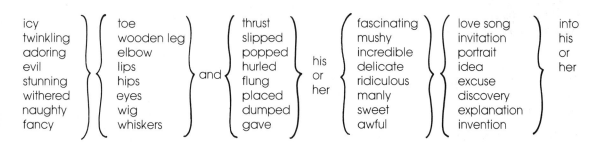

icy
twinkling
adoring
evil
stunning
withered
naughty
fancy
} {
toe
wooden leg
elbow
lips
hips
eyes
wig
whiskers
}
and
{
thrust
slipped
popped
hurled
flung
placed
dumped
gave
}
his
or
her
{
fascinating
mushy
incredible
delicate
ridiculous
manly
sweet
awful
}
{
love song
invitation
portrait
idea
excuse
discovery
explanation
invention
}
into
his
or
her

shy
funny
feeble
welcoming
hopeful
tearful
eager
empty
} {
mouth
arms
purse
pocket
hand
letter box
rubbish bin
handbag
}

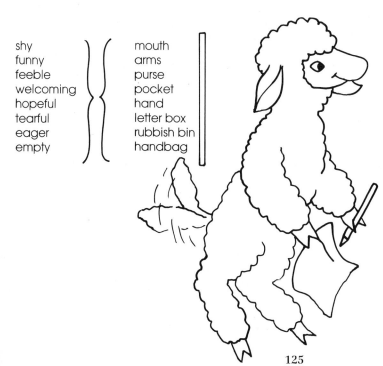

Become an instant Aussie author in two shakes of a lamb's tail. Choose a word from each column and — EUREKA! — you're home and hosed!

E.g. "Help!" sighed the nice bloke as the pitiful lover clasped his naughty whiskers and flung his mushy portrait into her welcoming handbag.

125

Because

1 Poets are more important than builders because _____

2 The sun rises because _____

3 Roses are red because _____

4 Teachers teach because _____

5 Frogs turn into Princes because _____

6 Tuesday is Tuesday because _____

7 We come to school because _____

8 Kittens grow into cats because _____

9 Bicycles should be banned because _____

10 It would be better if the moon shone during the day because _____

11 Milk comes in cartons or bottles because _____

12 Margarine rose to fame because _____

13 Kookaburras laugh because _____

14 Soccer is much better than football because _____

15 The Olympic Games may as well be cancelled from now on because _____

16 Spiders spin webs because _____

17 Humpty Dumpty sat on a wall because _____

18 Books should be made from very thin bark because _____

19 Birds eat worms because _____

20 People own pets because _____

21 Trains are much better than taxis because _____

22 Black is much prettier than red because _____

23 Aeroplanes were invented because _____

24 People die because _____

25 Grass grows because _____

26 Wars happen because _____

27 Dachshunds are l — o — n — g because _____

28 Cancel Christmas because _____

29 Fleas are smaller than elephants because _____

30 Beauty is more important than brains because _____

31 Brains are more important than beauty because _____

The Skull and the Skeleton   SHEET 10

Once a poor little orphan girl _____ forced to live with her old

_____ who ill-treated her and made her _____ her fingers to the

bone. From _____ minute she woke up in the _____ she was

made to scrub the _____ stone floors with a tiny brush, _____

clean the ancient stove, chop all _____ logs and the morning's wood

and _____ all the meals. She was dressed _____ rags and

tatters, was fed on _____ , and was made to sleep on _____

cobble-stones with only an old sack _____ a blanket. It was sadder

than _____ you could read about in the _____ storybooks.

    A day — a week — a year _____ . Time meant nothing to the

overworked, _____ girl, but there came a day _____ she could

take it no longer. _____ decided to run away. "Not that _____

have anywhere to run to; but _____ being eaten by wolves would be

_____ than staying here," she thought in _____ . She ran for hours,

now and _____ stopping, but then racing onwards. When _____

last she could run no longer, _____ stopped, gasping, and looked up.

She _____ standing in front of a big, _____ castle. It was so dark

and _____ that instinctively she felt something was _____ .

"All the same," she thought to _____ , "I have nowhere else to go

_____ I may as well knock. Perhaps _____ can take a job as a

_____ maid. I have had enough practice, _____ knows."

    She knocked on the door _____ — tap, tap . . . A light came on

_____ through a slit in the bars _____ could see a skull peering at

_____ . "What do you want?" it asked.

Can You Follow Instructions?   SHEET 11

1 Read everything before you do anything.

2 Put your name in the upper left-hand corner of this sheet.

3 Circle the *you* in number 1.

4 Draw four small circles in the upper right-hand corner of this sheet.

5 Put a √ in each circle mentioned in Number 4.

6 Put a square around one of the circles.

7 Write your age under the heading.

8 After the heading, write: *of course*!

9 Put a circle around sentence number 3.

10 Put an X in the lower right-hand corner of the sheet.

11 Draw a rectangle around the X you have just made.

12 On the back of this sheet, multiply 60 × 30.

13 Draw a square around the *sheet* in number 4.

14 Call out your teacher's name loudly when you get to this point.

15 If you think you have carefully followed the instructions, call out: "I have carefully followed the instructions".

16 On the back of this sheet, add 27 and 941.

17 Put a circle around your answer to number 16.

18 Count softly from one to ten.

19 Punch three holes with your pen here:

20 If you are the first one to get this far, call out: "I am the leader in following instructions".

21 Now that you have read this through carefully, do only question number 2.

Dot to Dot

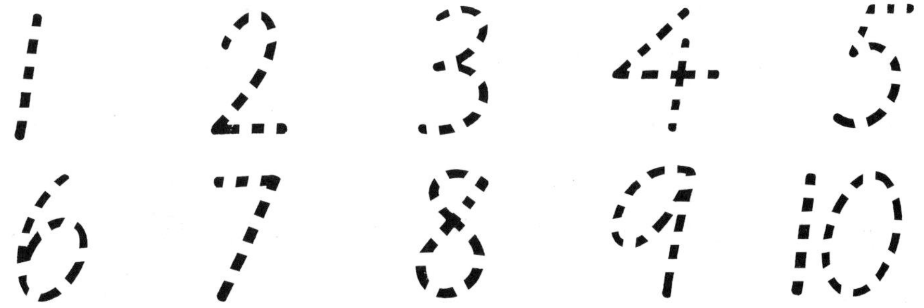

3•

2•

•4

•5

•6

7•

•8

•9

1•

10•

129

3 Frogs and 3 Snakes

Trace the numbers.

Circle the groups of three.

130

Which Tree Comes First?   SHEET 14

Colour by Number

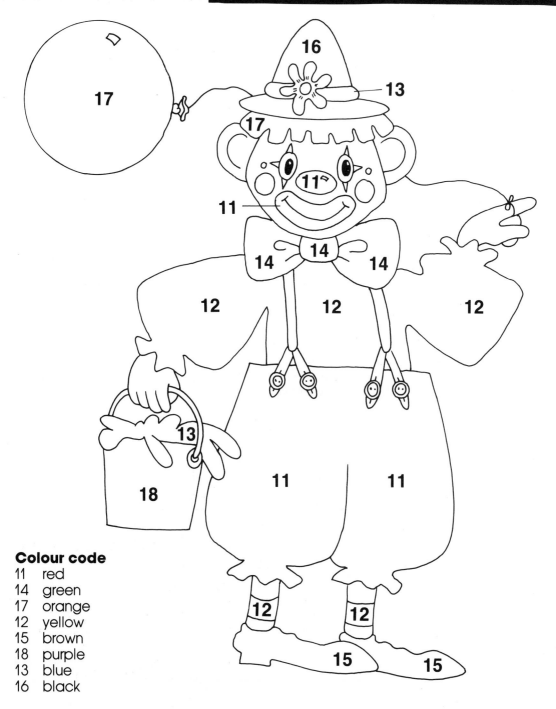

Colour code
11 red
14 green
17 orange
12 yellow
15 brown
18 purple
13 blue
16 black

132

Tangrams

Cut out this square and paste it onto a sheet of cardboard or coverpaper. When it is dry, cut it apart along the black lines. Then see how many pictures you can make with the seven pieces.

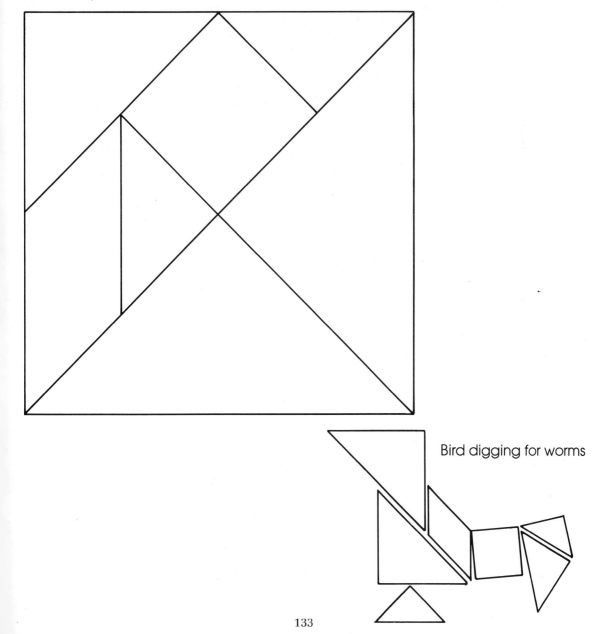

Bird digging for worms

Michael's Birthday Party

Colour Code

14	yellow	2	dark green	13	light brown
24	orange	15	dark brown	60	dark blue
17	grey	28	pink (skin)	5	dark green
21	light blue	40	red	6	black

134

Grandpa's Shortbread

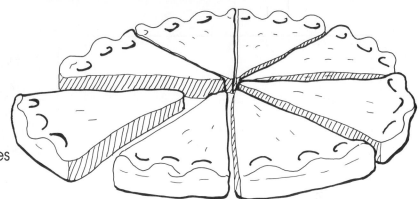

350g plain flour

Good pinch of salt

250g butter, softened

80g castor sugar

Extra sugar for sprinkling

Cooking time: 20 minutes

Oven: 170°C

Place flour in bowl with salt. Add butter, sugar and knead mixture into a ball. Turn onto a lightly floured board and shape into a round. Flour the rolling pin and roll mixture out to about 1 cm thick. Cut into rounds and place on a baking tray. Sprinkle lightly with sugar and bake in oven for 15–20 minutes.

A   Look closely at Grandpa's shortbread recipe.

   i   What is the weight of the sugar and butter together?

   ii   What is the difference in weight between the flour and the butter?

   iii   What is the total weight of the flour, butter and sugar?

B   Choose from the weights drawn here to show the following amounts.

   i   200g   ii   50g   iii   350g

   iv   400g

C   If you doubled the quantity of Grandpa's Shortbread, that would be enough for the whole grade. Write out the recipe for double the quantity.

The Mysterious 34's

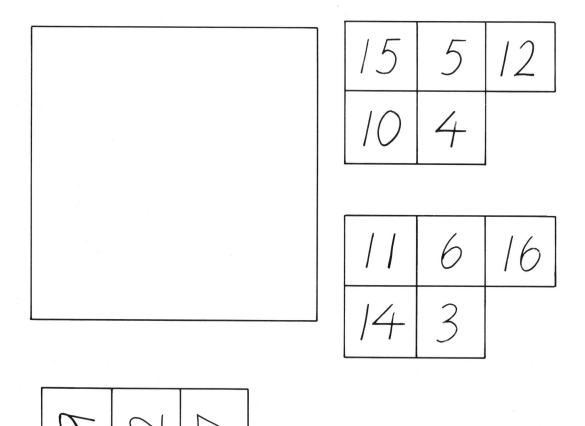

Cut out these five shapes, then try to fit the four smaller ones onto the large square.
Can you arrange them so that the numbers will total 34, not only up, down, across and
diagonally, but also so that the four numbers in each quarter of the square will total
34?
There are three ways of fitting the shapes into the square, but only one is correct.

136

Mysterious Treasure Hunt

1 100 less than 2050

2 The difference between 100 and 64

4 Arrange from smallest to largest: $\frac{1}{5}$ $\frac{1}{3}$ $\frac{1}{4}$ $\frac{1}{2}$ $\frac{7}{8}$

8 $100 - \frac{1}{6}$ of 60

3 769 $\times$ 6

5 $2\frac{1}{4} + 1\frac{3}{8}$

6 $615 \div 8$

9 How many days in Autumn?

7 Days in 9 years

12 $7040 \div 20$

10 2 metres. How many millimetres?

11 $2 \times 73 \times 6$

13 Product of 40 and 50

14 $1\frac{1}{2}$ kg of cheese @ \$5.70/kg

16 Gold coins worth \$24,000. How many, if each is worth \$1000?

15 \$98.14 in words

18 652 $\times$ 0

17 652×1

EUREKA!

19 Compass direction from this stepping stone to treasure chest:

137

Test Score Board

WEST INDIES First Innings		AUSTRALIA First Innings	
	Runs		
G. GREENIDGE, c Hogg, b Lawson	95	G. WOOD, c Greenidge, b Harper	41
D. HAYNES, c Hughes, b Hogg	0	J. DYSON, c Dujon, b Walsh	8
R. RICHARDSON, c Border, b Lawson	8	K. WESSELS, b Marshall	98
L. GOMES, c Rixon b Lawson	60	S. RIXON, c Richards, b Marshall	0
V. RICHARDS, c Rixon, b Lawson	0	K. HUGHES, c Dujon, b Garner	0
C. LLOYD, b Lawson	78	A. BORDER, c Garner, b Marshall	21
J. DUJON, lbw, b Lawson	77	D. BOON, c Dujon, b Marshall	12
M. MARSHAL, c Rixon, b Lawson	9	G. LAWSON, c Dujon, b Garner	49
R. HARPER, c Rixon, b Lawson	9	R. HOLLAND, c Haynes, b Walsh	2
J. GARNER, not out	8	R. HOGG, not out	7
C. WALSH, b Holland	0	T. ALDERMAN, c Richardson, b Marshall	
Sundries (5b, 4lb, 3nb)	12	....	10
TOTAL		Sundries (2b, 8lb, 26nb)	36
		TOTAL	

1 What was the West Indies first innings total?

2 What was the Australians first innings total?

3 By how many runs did the West Indies lead Australia on the first innings?

4 Who was the top scorer for each side?

5 How many more runs did Greenidge make than the second top West Indies scorer?

6 If Wood's other innings so far had been 14, 0, 28, 7, 48, and 10, what would his average be now?

7 If the West Indies made 244 in their second innings, how many runs would Australia have to make to win the test?

8 What was the combined total of sundries scored by the two sides in their first innings?

138

Space Patrol

1   $4^2 + 6 \times 5 + 2 = \ldots\ldots$
2   $\frac{1}{2}$ of $100 + 2 \times 2 = \ldots\ldots$
3   2 dozen plus eight $= \ldots\ldots$
4   $400 - 20 \times 20 + 1 = \ldots\ldots$
5   $9 \times 12 + 674 \times 0 = \ldots\ldots$

6   $(24 \div 2) + 10 \times 8 + 4 = \ldots\ldots$
7   $4 + 4 + 4 + 4 = \ldots\ldots$
8   $360 \div 6 = \ldots\ldots$
9   $1\,\text{m} + 16\,\text{cm} = \ldots\ldots$ cm

Colour code

116 dark blue	48 pink	16 light brown
1 orange	32 red	60 black
54 yellow	108 dark blue	96 light green

139

Shared Shapes

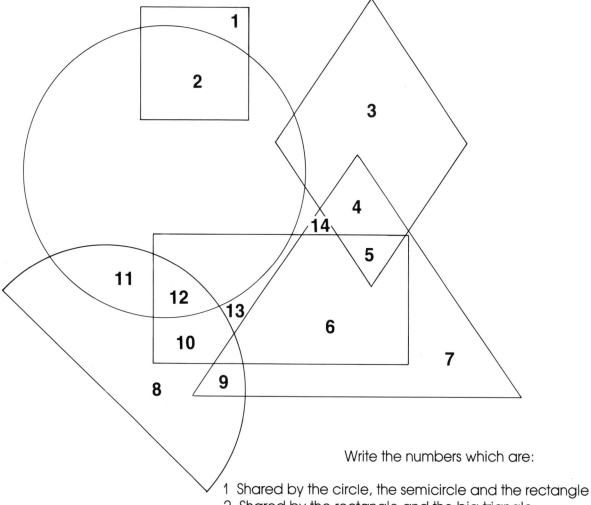

Write the numbers which are:

1 Shared by the circle, the semicircle and the rectangle
2 Shared by the rectangle and the big triangle
3 In the circle, but not in the semicircle
4 In the circle, but not in the square
5 Shared by the big triangle and the diamond
6 In the semicircle only
7 Shared by the rectangle and the diamond
8 In the diamond and the big triangle
9 Shared by the circle and the square
10 In the square but not in the circle

Make up your own number p

140

Make Your Own Flag

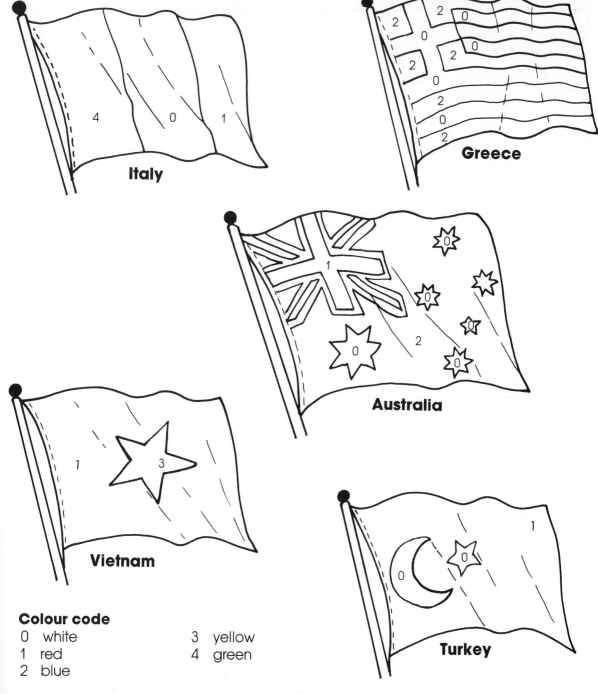

Italy

Greece

Australia

Vietnam

Turkey

Colour code

0	white	3	yellow
1	red	4	green
2	blue		

141

Positively Ozitively Answer Sheet

Name the capital cities of . . .

VICTORIA _____

N.S.W. _____

W.A. _____

N.T. _____

TAS. _____

QLD. _____

S.A. _____

Write rhymes for

damper _____

digger _____

bloke _____

shearer _____

mare _____

wattle _____

billy _____

FILL
THIS
GAP

The bunyip leered at me. Terrified, I _____

_____

_____

What are? Who are?

Buffalo _____

Henry Lawson _____

Ned Kelly _____

The Murray _____

Kosciusko _____

Ayers or Hanging _____

Australia II _____

Banjo Paterson _____

Donald Bradman _____

Burke & Wills _____

Menzies (Robert) _____

Pharlap _____

Eucalypts _____

Countdown _____

Holden _____

Write 2 famous Australian people.

_____

_____

Write 2 famous Australian places.

_____

_____

Write 4 famous Australian animals.

_____

_____

Write 1 famous Australian pop group.

Design a new flag for Australia.

On the back of this sheet, make as many words as you can from the word BUSHRANGER.

Write as many aboriginal place names as you can fit in this space (use an atlas if you wish).

Dinkum Aussie Passport

SELF PORTRAIT
(head only)

YOUR NAME _____
AGE _____ **BIRTHDAY** _____
ADDRESS _____
_____

List the people who live in your house — including
pets. Give ages of children — but not the age of
adults. _____
_____
_____

I feel happy when

_____
_____
_____

I feel sad when

_____
_____
_____

My favourite day is

I WAS BORN IN
(place)

_____

MUM WAS BORN IN
(place)

_____

DAD WAS BORN IN
(place)

_____

**DESCRIPTION OF
YOU**
height _____
eye colour _____
hair colour _____
scars _____

WHERE WOULD YOU LIKE TO GO FOR A HOLIDAY?
* **Inside Australia** _____

* **Outside Australia** _____

**THUMB
PRINT**

Things you like (food, sport,
hobbies, pop groups, TV shows)

Things you don't like

143

Crack the Code

In the 1500's an Italian named Giovanni Porta designed a code based on a framework of squares and dots. Here is the code:

Make up some codes of your own to try on your friends, parents or teachers.

A ⌙   B ⌐⌙   C .⌙   D ⊔   E ⊔   F ⌙.

G ⌊   H ⌊   I ⌊.   J ⌐   K ⌐   L ⌐.

M ☐   N ☐   O ⌊.   P ⌐   Q ⌐   R ⌐.

S ⌐   T ⌐   U .⌐   V ⌐   W ⌐   X ⌐.

So the message *Crack the Code* would be written as:

Y ⌐⌐   Z ⌐⌐

.⌊. ⌙ .⌙ ⌐   ⌐⌊⊔   .⊔⊔⊔

Can you answer this coded question?

⌐ ⌊⌊. .⌙⌊ ⌊⌐ ⊔⌐⌐⌊⊔⌊. ⌙

⌐⌊. ⌐☐ ⊔⊔ ⊔⊔⌐⌐⌊⊔⌊⌐ ⌊.⌊.

⌙ ⌐⌊⌐☐ ⊔⊔ ⌊⌐⌐⊔ ?

Make up your own Porta code for this:
Question: Why was the teacher cross-eyed?
Answer: Because she couldn't control her pupils!

Make up some codes of your own to try on your friends, parents or teachers.

144

Build on a Shape

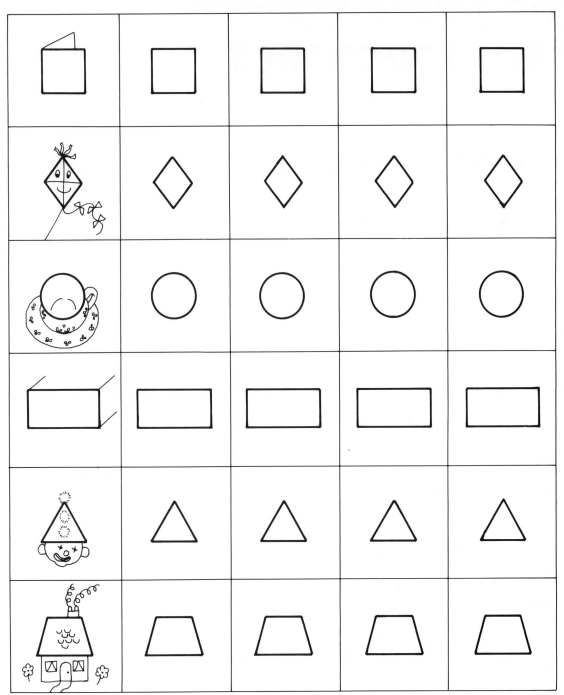

Faded Proverbs

FADED PROVERBS

A STITCH IN TIME SAVES NINE.

THE EARLY BIRD CATCHES THE WORM.

ONE GOOD TURN DESERVES ANOTHER.

LET SLEEPING DOGS LIE.

GREAT MINDS THINK ALIKE.

Is it a Flying Saucer . . . Is It a Donut?   SHEET 30

147

Top Notch Tasketition

NAME _____

Design a cover for a small book this size. Include the title:

Draw something in this circle.

Whose beady eyes are staring at you? Complete this picture — by making an unusual creature and naming it.

◎ ◎

FILL THE GAPS

This morning I _____ found that my _____ had _____ .

Unfortunately _____ _____

so I thought to myself ____ _____

A DO-IT YOURSELF POEM

Oh, if _____ feeling _____
Or, if you're _____
Why don't you _____
Or maybe even _____

W H Y ?

WRITE A NEW WORD TO EXPRESS VERY GREAT EXCITEMENT

_____

DECORATIVE S

In olden days, the first letter of a word in a paragraph was beautifully decorated with trailing plants, ferns, creatures — all kinds of things, like this O. You try one for S — perhaps for a story 'Seasons of Sorrows'. Draw a large decoratives S — then add suitable embellishments.

INITIALS

Use your own initials to do this kind of thing: V.F. (Virginia Ferguson) = Very Funny — Verifying Falsehoods
P.D. (Peter Durkin) = Perfect Design
Now do yours, then do some of your friends.

_____
_____
_____
_____

Which Word Is Out?

Underline the odd word out in each group and say why.
There are more than one or two answers to some of the questions, e.g. *Bill, Fred, Eric, Ted.*
The answer could be *Ted* — because all the others have four letters; it could be *Bill,* because his name is the only one without an E; it could be Eric, because his name is out of alphabetical order . . . Get the idea?

1 Kosciusko, Buffalo, Blue Mountains, Ben Nevis _____

2 tomato, potato, carrot, peas _____

3 kookaburra, lyrebird, rosella, storks _____

4 chooks, planes, hang-gliders, parachutes _____

5 Brisbane, Bundaberg, Bairnsdale, Perth _____

6 ape, gorilla, jaguar, man _____

7 peep, stare, glare, poke _____

8 rectangle, square, triangle, oval _____

9 gum, wattle, bottlebrush, tulips _____

10 step mother, step ladder, step father, step daughter _____

11 F, A, E, I _____

12 December, April, January, February _____

13 moan, groan, sigh, frown _____

14 icecream, chocolates, cheese, lollies _____

15 midnight, 6 + 6 = , dozen, mid-week _____

16 wind, rain, hail, snow _____

149

Colour The Rainbow

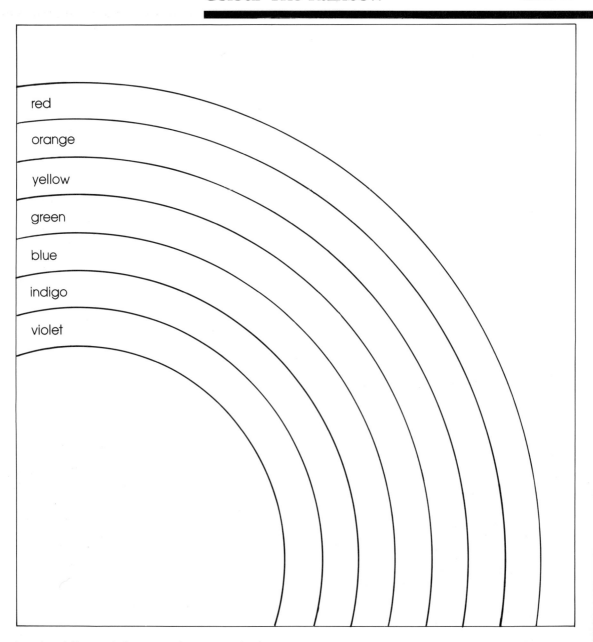

red

orange

yellow

green

blue

indigo

violet

Look at the rainbow colour words.

Colour in the rainbow, then cut it out and paste it onto a larger sheet.

Draw a picture around your rainbow.

The Three Billy Goats Gruff

Creative Colouring In   I

152

You Be the Artist

Eight Art

Colour some shapes to make patterns of eight.

154

Draw a Dinosaur

Here is an easy way for you to draw a dinosaur. Look closely at the drawing. Each square in the drawing is numbered. The same number appears in the empty squares below. If you copy the parts of the dinosaur in each numbered square, your drawing should closely resemble the smaller picture.

When you have completed this sheet, you can experiment with other drawings. Find a small picture and pencil numbered squares over it. Then draw larger squares onto a blank sheet of paper.
This method is especially useful for drawing enlarged copies of maps.

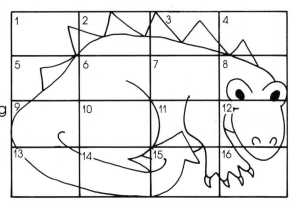

1	2	3	4
5	6	7	8
9	10	11	12
13	14	15	16

155

Creative Colouring In   II

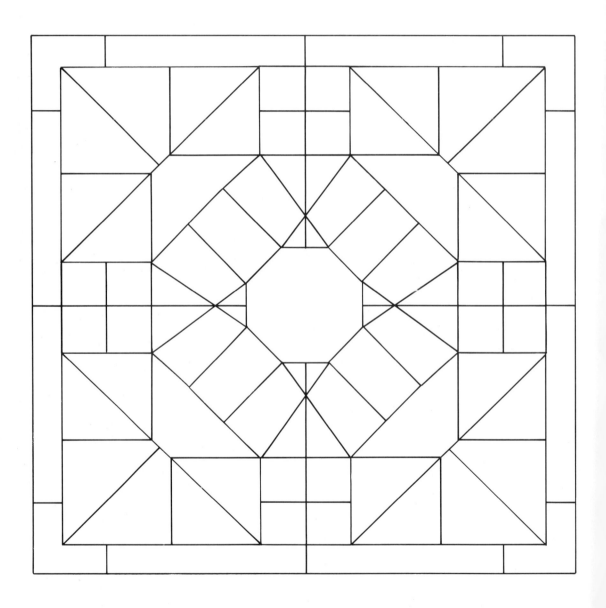

157

5 Literature

This chapter was, for us, a daunting task. The scope and field of children's literature is broad: we couldn't decide what to leave out, let alone what to leave in! Both of us have worked with books and children for donkeys' years, and there is so much to tell. Such beautiful picture books, novels and unforgettable stories, and so many. How could we possibly encapsulate forty years of teaching experience into fifty pages? We couldn't.

So we divided this chapter into three sections — stories, books and poems. We have included detailed poetry lesson plans for junior, middle and upper levels, but we have space only to include annotations of our favourite stories and books. It is essential to begin your own collections. Ask for children's books for birthday or Christmas presents. Visit libraries and bookshops often in order to familiarise yourself with children's books.

Stories

By stories we mean short stories which are complete within themselves and which usually take from ten to twenty minutes to read or to tell.

These are some story collections which we couldn't do without:

To Read and To Tell and *More Stories To Read and to Tell* edited by Norah Montgomerie (Bodley Head).

Stories for Tens and Over edited by Sara and Stephen Corrin, (Puffin). If you bought the set of these books: *Stories for the Under Fives, Stories for Five Year Olds, Sixes . . . Sevens . . . Eights . . . Nines . . . Tens and Over*, you would have enough stories to last you for years.

A Book of Giants edited by Ruth Manning-Sanders. Also *A Book of Dragons, A Book of Witches, A Book of Ghosts*, and many other titles (Piccolo).

Tales From Grimm, by Wanda Gag (Faber). *The Faber Book of Stories, The Faber Storybook, The Faber Book of Nursery Stories* (Faber).

Keep an eye open for contemporary Australian collections: *Too True* (Tall stories) edited by Anne Ingram (Collins). Also *Shudders and Shakes*.

The Pickled Boeing, an excellent collection edited by Anne Ingram. (Children's Medical Foundation).

Ratbags and Rascals — funny stories by Robin Klein (Dent).

Which particular stories from those collections do we recommend? Tastes (yours, ours and the children's) vary, but these stories nearly always work:

Old favourites like *The Tale of a Turnip* and *The Three Billy Goats Gruff* are still enjoyed, even though you will always get the Grade 1 sceptic who will call out, "We *know* that one! We've heard it before!" Our standard reply to this is, "Well, aren't you lucky, now you're going to hear it *again* — in a different way — *my* way!"

Story	Level (a rough guide)
The Six Servants, from *Tales From Grimm* by Wanda Gag (Faber).	All
The Lion Hunt, from *Juba This and Juba That* (Little, Brown). Our version is in this book on pages 9–11.	J
The Princess of Tomboso, from *The Magic Tree* (Scholastic). Reprinted in this book on pages 67–73.	M U
The Seventeen Oranges, from *The Goalkeeper's Revenge* by Bill Naughton (Puffin).	All
Mollie Whuppie, from *The Faber Book of Nursery Stories*. This retelling — by Walter de la Mare — is our favourite version of this story for telling.	J M
Where Arthur Sleeps from *Welsh Folk Tales* (O.U.P).	U
The Golden Leg, from *Juba This and Juba That* (Little, Brown).	U
The Hairy Toe, from *Watch Out for Witches* (Nelson).	All
The Yellow Ribbon, from *Watch Out for Witches* (Nelson).	All
The Hobyahs, from the *Grade 2 Reader* (Education Department of Victoria).	J
The Schnooks Family, from *Juba This and Juba That* (Little, Brown).	J
Caps for Sale by Esphyr Slobodkina (Scholastic)	J
J. Roodie, from *Ratbags and Rascals* by Robin Klein (Dent). Reprinted in this book on pages 103–105.	All
The Skull and the Skeleton, (from one of the Ruth Manning-Sanders collections, but we prefer our tongue-in-cheek version in *Danger* (Young Australia Readers, Nelson)	U

That's only a handful to go on with: you will need to read hundreds of stories before you are able to make your own Top Ten or Twenty lists.

We have told these stories to mixed groups from Preps to Grade 6 and we find it hard to put age levels on most of them. We had always considered *The Princess of Tomboso* a long and convoluted story, far too difficult for young children, but last year at Rosevern, it was our Grade 1's favourite story.

So don't be put off by our symbols; if you really enjoy a story it will usually work at any level.

Books

Here are some of our favourite books at the different levels. We have chosen books which have (mostly) stood the test of time, rather than the very newest publications.

JUNIOR LEVEL

Are You My Mother?
P.D. Eastman   (Collins)
A tiny bird searches through every nook and cranny to find his mother, but finally, with the aid of "Snort", the mechanical monster, he arrives back home and his mission is fulfilled.

Bears in the Night
Stan and Jan Berenstain   (Collins)
Simple words and mysterious night-time illustrations show the bears' adventures.

Caps For Sale
Esphyr Slobodkina   (Scholastic)
A Tale of a Peddler, Some Monkeys, and Their Monkey Business. The Monkeys steal the sleeping peddler's caps, but he tricks them into giving them back.

The Fat Cat
Jack Kent   (Puffin)
Tongue-in-cheek cumulative folk tale about the cat who swallowed everyone he met — until the woodcutter came by.

Frederick
Leo Lionni   (Andersen Press)
Gentle collage illustrations match this poetic story of a mouse who hoards poems and thoughts (instead of food) to tide him over the long winter months.

Harry the Dirty Dog
Gene Zion   (Puffin)
The first title in the series which includes: *Harry and the Lady Next Door; No Roses for Harry.*

The Magic Pasta Pot
Tomie De Paola   (Andersen Press)
A cumulative tale from Italy about Grandma Witch and her magic pasta pot.

Meg and Mog
Helen Nicoll   (Puffin)
Very simple storyline but striking illustrations in clear bright colours (Jan Pienkowski) appeal to all children. Many titles: *Meg at Sea; Meg's Eggs; Meg on the Moon*

Mr. Gumpy's Outing
John Burningham   (Puffin)
Each animal is allowed to come on the outing IF . . . Of course they all do the wrong thing — and they all end up in the river.
Also: *Mr. Gumpy's Motor Car*

Noisy Nora
Rosemary Wells   (Collins)
No one notices Nora when she is noisy, so she tries keeping quiet.
Also: *Benjamin and Tulip*

Rosie's Walk
Pat Hutchins   (Puffin)
Rosie's adventuring takes her over, under, up, through, between, across and past the entire farmyard, until her terrifying encounter with the fox . . .

Terry's Brrrmmm G T
Ted Greenwood   (Scholastic)

George and Terry work hard to make their extra-special billycart. At last it is the day for the Great Race. Also: *V.I.P.* (about a very important plant).

The Truck on the Track
Janet Burroway   (Piccolo)
Lively illustrations by J.V. Lord match the rhyming text in this cumulative story which ends with a splendid and satisfying collision.

The Very Hungry Caterpillar
Eric Carle   (Puffin)
A tiny, very hungry caterpillar eats his way through brightly colored pages and many enticing foods. Also: *1, 2, 3 to the Zoo; Do You Want To Be My Friend?*

Where the Wild Things Are
Maurice Sendak   (Puffin)
Max was sent to his room without any supper, so he sailed off to the land where the wild things are. When he cooled off and sailed back home, his supper was waiting — "and it was still hot". A modern classic with superb illustrations.

Whistle for Willie
Ezra Jack Keats   (Puffin)
A little boy learns to whistle — and his family celebrate. Also: *Pet Show; Apt. 3; Louie's Lot; Hi, Cat!; Goggles; Peter's Chair*

Who Sank the Boat?
Pamela Allen   (Nelson)
One warm sunny morning some good friends decided to go for a row in the bay. The cow, the donkey, the sheep and the pig climbed on board, but there was one more to go . . . Readers have to wait till the very end to find out who sank the boat.

MIDDLE LEVEL

Anno's Alphabet
M. Anno   (Bodley Head)
Subtitled "an adventure in imagination" this work of art will appeal to all ages.
Also: *Anno's Journey* — a book without words which will inspire much lively discussion.
Also: *Anno's Animals* — which are hidden in the pictures.

Arabel's Raven
Joan Aiken   (BBC/Jackanory)
The world's most outrageous raven, Mortimer can eat five pints of milk and one pound of sausages for a meal — with a flight of stairs for dessert! But Arabel loves her new pet and pushes him around in her block-trolley. Illustrated by Quentin Blake. Also: *Mortimer's Tie*

Badjelly the Witch
Spike Milligan   (Michael Joseph/Target)
A great favorite with nearly all children. They all love the cat with the special name — Fluffybum!

Bedtime for Frances
Russell Hoban   (Puffin)
Children of this age love to talk about the things they did when they were the same age as Frances.
Also: *A Baby Sister for Frances*

Bottersnikes and Gumbles
S.A. Wakefield   (Collins)
A zany ecological fantasy about the creatures that live in the tip — the amiable Gumbles and their lazy enemies, the Bottersnikes. Illustrated by Desmond Digby.

A Boy, a Dog, and a Frog
Mercer Mayer   (Collins)
An engaging adventure without words which appeals to all ages and abilities. Many titles in this series but this one is the best.

Captain Pugwash
John Ryan   (Puffin)
Captain Pugwash thought he was the bravest pirate on the seven seas, but where would he have been without Tom (the cabin boy) — especially when dastardly Cut-Throat Jake appeared?
Many titles in the series.

Casey, the Utterly Impossible Horse
Anita Feagles   (Puffin)
Tall tale about a horse who wants a boy of his own.

Charlie and the Chocolate Factory
Roald Dahl   (Puffin)
One of the most popular books in primary school libraries. Also: *The Magic Finger; Danny, the Champion of the World; Fantastic Mr Fox*

Charlotte's Web
E.B. White   (Puffin)
This modern classic about Wilbur the pig and Charlotte the spider is a philosophical novel in which one friend dies for another. All ages.

The Day the Space Ship Landed
Beman Lord   (Nelson)
Ten-year-old Mike finds a space ship in his backyard. Also: *The Space Ship Returns*

Flat Stanley
Jeff Brown   (Methuen)
Stanley is flattened by a falling notice-board, but he learns to live with his disability. Zany illustrations by Tomi Ungerer.

Giant Devil Dingo
Dick Roughsey   (Collins)
With glowing earthy colours the author/artist presents a genuine Aboriginal legend about the evil old Eelgin, the grasshopper woman, and her giant devil dingo, Gaiya.

Gobbolino the Witch's Cat
Ursula M. Williams   (Puffin)

Gobbolino didn't want to learn spells. He wanted to be loved and to belong to a family — so he defected. A warm story.

Jim and the Beanstalk
Raymond Briggs   (Puffin)
An up-dated and very funny picture book version of Jack . . .

John Brown, Rose and the Midnight Cat
Jenny Wagner   (Puffin)
John Brown, the Old English Sheepdog, and Rose had been together for a long time, and they were very happy — until the Midnight Cat arrived.
Also: *The Bunyip of Berkeley's Creek*
Both have beautiful illustrations by Ron Brooks.

Little Old Mrs Pepperpot
Alf Prøysen   (Puffin)
Mrs Pepperpot has the strange habit of shrinking at the most unexpected times. Many titles in the series.

McBroom's Wonderful One-acre Farm
Sid Fleischman   (Puffin)
Happy tall-tale of the irrepressible Josh McBroom and his eleven red-headed children.
Also: *McBroom Tells a Lie*

The Oath of Bad Brown Bill
Steve Axelsen   (Puffin)
Humorous ballad about a boastful bushranger, his horse Mudpie and the dread Pale Jackeroo. Picture book.

The Pie-Makers
Helen Cresswell   (Puffin)
Piemaking is the finest vocation in the world — according to Gravella's family. (She would have been named Gravy, if she'd been a boy!) A delightful, funny fantasy.
Also: *The Nightwatchmen; The Signposters*

The Three Robbers
Tomi Ungerer   (Methuen)

Three fierce robbers capture a little girl called Tiffany — by mistake!
Also: *Zeralda's Ogre*, about the importance of being well-fed.
Also: *The Beast of Monsieur Racine; The Hat*

The 27th Annual African Hippopotamus Race
Morris Lurie   (Puffin)
A very funny spoof about Australia's obsession with the training of swimming champions — set in the African jungle! Also *Toby's Millions*

UPPER LEVEL

Adrift
Allan Baillie   (Nelson)
Flynn, Sally and their cat Nebu are alone on the raft and drifting further and further from the shore. There is no way that they can return to safety. The book was inspired by a news item about four boys and a dog adrift on an old packing case in the Mediterranean.

Bridge to Terabithia
Katherine Paterson   (Puffin)
Newbery Award winner. A powerful and moving story, impossible to sum up in a few lines.
Also: *Jacob Have I Loved; The Sign of the Chrysanthemum*; and *The Great Gilly Hopkins*

The Cay
Theodore Taylor   (Puffin)
Two shipwrecked people struggle for survival on a small Carribean island. Changing relationships between the blind boy and the old Negro are developed with sensitivity.

Encyclopedia Brown . . . (series)
Donald J. Sobol   (Nelson/Ashton Schol.)
A ten-year-old detective solves mysteries which are too hard for his father, the Chief of Police. One mystery to each chapter — with solutions.
Many titles in the series.

Finn Family Moomintroll
Tove Jansson   (Puffin)
Fantasies from Finland about a very special family of Moomins (a kind of troll). Their adventures are wise, human, sometimes sad, often funny and always hopeful. Many titles in the series.

Fly-By-Night
K.M. Peyton   (Sparrow)
A girl who yearns for a horse finds it is not as easy as she had hoped. Continued in: *The Team*.
Also: *Flambards* (series); *The Beethoven Medal*

Fungus the Bogeyman
Raymond Briggs   (Nelson)
Everything you ever wanted to know (and some you probably didn't) about bogeymen. A comic-strip encyclopedia, very popular with most ages.

Grinny
Nicholas Fisk   (Puffin)
Easy-to-read science fiction, told in diary form. Grinny appears from nowhere and says she is Great Aunt Emma. Tim and Beth realise she is dangerous.

Horned Helmet
Henry Treece   (Puffin)
Beorn, an Icelandic boy, joins a crew of fierce Vikings.

Also: *Viking's Dawn; The Road to Miklagaard; Viking's Sunset*

How to Eat Fried Worms
Thomas Rockwell   (Collins)
A funny, easy-to-read book about real children. Fried worm recipes included!
Also: *The Neon Motorcycle* — about a boy who falls from a window and Just Happens to land on a Harley Davidson motor bike.

The Incredible Steam-Driven Adventures of Riverboat Bill

Cliff Green   (Hodder)
A rollicking saga with a larger-than-life cast.

The Iron Man
Ted Hughes   (Faber)
A short but powerful and poetic novel in which friendship and trust overcome fear and suspicion.

Midnite
Randolph Stow   (Puffin)
Witty send-up of The Australian Bushranger. Captain Midnite, good looking but not bright, is supported by his faithful gang (which includes a cat and a cockatoo) until he eventually becomes the richest man in the colony.

My Side of the Mountain
Jean George   (Puffin)
A city boy decides to get away from the rat race and live alone in the wild Catskill Mountains.

The Nargun and the Stars
Patricia Wrightson   (Puffin)
A brilliant Australian fantasy. The Nargun was older than time. As it moved relentlessly down the mountain, Simon and his family fought back with the ancient magic of the land.
Continued in: *The Ice is Coming*
Also: *An Older Kind of Magic; The Rocks of Honey*

Nightbirds on Nantucket
Joan Aiken   (Puffin)
Dido Twite, an amazing heroine, experiences adventures involving smugglers, witches, fire, wolves, kidnapping, exposure, shipwreck — you name it! Other energetic historical fantasies include: *Black Hearts in Battersea; The Wolves of Willoughby Chase; The Cuckoo Tree*

Patatrac
J. Loup   (Cape)

A book without words. A brilliant book of disasters, full of detail and exciting incident.

For all ages.

Penny Pollard's Diary
Robin Klein   (Oxford)
Penny Pollard hates schools, elderly citizens, pink dresses and Mondays, but when she meets old Mrs Bettany on a school excursion her outlook gradually changes.

The Phantom Tollbooth
Norton Juster   (Collins Lion)
Milo, the hero, is bored — but not for long. His toll-booth leads him to odd lands where words and numbers don't behave in the usual way. Maths people like this book.

The Shrinking of Treehorn
Florence P. Heide   (Puffin)
Treehorn, a small boy, is shrinking — but no-one believes him. A delightful predicament, illustrated by Edward Gorey.

The Silver Crown
Robert C. O'Brien   (Collins Lion)
Ellen finds a crown on her pillow, and her life is never the same.
Also: *Mrs Frisby and the Rats of Nimh* — a rare and sensitive fantasy.

Smith
Leon Garfield   (Puffin)
A 12 year-old pickpocket in 18th Century London.
Also: *Black Jack; Devil-in-the-Fog; Jack Holborn; The Sound of Coaches*

The Turbulent Term of Tyke Tiler
Gene Kemp   (Puffin)
Energetic Tyke is one of the busiest, fastest and most mischievous people in the school.

If you want more detailed annotations or longer lists, look at:

* *Books for Children*, The Children's Book Council list — available from some bookshops or from the Council — Box 2428V, G.P.O. Melbourne 3001.

* *Happily Ever After* — Supplement to the Literature Guide, published by the Education Department of Victoria.

* *Read All About It: Books to read for all ages*, by V. Ferguson, published by The Educational Clearinghouse P.O. Box 249, E. Melbourne, 3002.

* The Australian Library Promotion Council, 328 Swanston St., Melbourne (Ph. 63–5994) produces many very good lists e.g. *Funny Bones to Make You Laugh, How to Get Your Child to Read, Ring Around the World* (folk tales) . . . and many more.

Poetry

Poetry for children has changed dramatically since *The Book of 1000 Poems*. Today there are hundreds of new and exciting poetry collections. No *one* collection will suit every teacher, so we recommend that you find a large basic anthology such as *Time For Poetry*, edited by May Hill Arbuthnot (Scott-Foresman), and then, to begin with, select one or two from the following list. Oxford University Press in London has produced four excellent poetry anthologies containing many fresh poems. These are titled simply *A First Poetry Book, A Second Poetry Book, A Third Poetry Book* and *A Fourth Poetry Book*.
Now, Oxford in Australia has produced a similar set: *A First Australian Poetry Book, A Second Australian Poetry Book, A Third Australian Poetry Book* and *A Fourth Australian Poetry Book*. Those eight books could form a sound basis for any teacher's personal collection.

* *The Faber Book of Nursery Verse*, edited by Barbara Ireson (Faber), is another versatile anthology. Don't be put off by the word *nursery* — there are poems for all ages here, although it caters particularly well for children at the Junior and Middle levels.

* *Bullseyes*, edited by Brian Thompson (Longman), is another winner: the poems are all excellent and the design and illustration are beautiful.

Funny Poems

You can always win children by using funny poems and rhymes. The famous foursome — *Oh, How Silly!, Beastly Boys and Ghastly Girls, Oh, That's Ridiculous!,* and *Oh, What Nonsense!* — edited by William Cole and illustrated by Tomi Ungerer (Methuen), have been around for a long time.

Keep an eye open for new collections of humorous poems by *real* poets, not just rhymesters.
* *Hot Dog* by Kit Wright (Puffin)
* *Rabbiting On* by Kit Wright (Collins)
* *Mind Your Own Business* by Michael Rosen (Collins)
* *A Light in the Attic* and *Where the Sidewalk Ends* by Shel Silverstein (Harper and Row)

Also try new paperbacks featuring many different poets, such as
* *Poems for Fun* (Beaver)
* *Ducks and Dragons* (Puffin)
* *Gangsters, Ghosts and Dragonflies* — a book of story poems edited by Brian Patten (Piccolo).

Poems that Can't Fail

Most of the poems in this section are poems which can be acted out. In the beginning, to be certain of succeeding with poetry, you really need to involve the children physically so that, in their re-enactment or performance, they make the poems come alive.

The poems here are ones we've tried with all age groups, and which have been more successful than others in our repertoire. We've made an arbitrary division between Junior, Middle and Upper to make it easier for you. Except for the very youngest (e.g. *The Moo-Cow-Moo*) and the oldest (e.g. *Silent Hill*) most of the poems could be used at any level — depending upon whether or not you feel comfortable with them, and whether the children are in the right frame of mind.

We have included short commentaries, methods of presentation and ideas for activities for each poem.

Remember, though, that the final choice is up to you: the sky's the limit, and a poem can lead you anywhere!

JUNIOR LEVEL

Bushrangers

Fifty burly bushrangers
   Went out to steal some gold;
But all the bush was wet with dew
   And one caught a cold.
And one found a bulldog ant
   Creeping on his chest;
And one had a 'gammy' leg
   And had to have a rest.
One thought he saw a snake,
   Another had a pain;
The rest, they heard a gun go off,
   And scampered home again.

Isobel Kendall Bowden

Children really enjoy this moderately boisterous rhyme. To begin, ask for volunteers to become fifty burly bushrangers. This means that all children will be involved.
Select five who will develop various ailments during the performance.
Begin reading the poem, with both teacher and children stomping through the *quiet*

undergrowth, in rhythm to the words. When you come to line four, point to Ailing Bushranger 1 who coughs, splutters and falls to the ground. The rest of the class stomp around for a short time until you read lines five and six, when Ailing Bushranger 2 scratches with horror and falls to the ground as the bulldog ant creeps on his chest.
In the same way Bushranger 3 limps along and falls down (you may need to explain *gammy leg*). Bushranger 4 shivers with fear and hides behind something on the ground and Number 5 grimaces with pain, holds his side and subsides quietly.
The rest of the children begin to stomp around again, but as you read the words *a gun go off* make a loud banging noise and they all race to hide behind a table, chair, bench cupboard, door — or whatever.
Choose five different actors for each rendition.

from Fish fingers

If you hold a shell to your ear, they say,
   You'll hear the sea winds blow.
I held one to my ear. It said:
   "Ullo, 'ullo, 'ullo.'

Max Fatchen

Use a large shell, or an empty tin (which you pretend is a shell).
Say the first three lines of the rhyme with the shell held to your ear, but for the last line move the shell to your mouth and say in an oceany-echoey voice, "Ullo, ullo, ullo".

Variation
Choose a child, repeat the first two lines, then say *Anna held one up to her ear* (Hand shell to Anna.) *It said* (and Anna says, holding the shell to her mouth) "Ullo, ullo, ullo". Give at least five children a turn.

Some of our more polite students find it very hard to say "Ullo". In their very best telephone voices, they croon "Hellooo."
One Grade 2 brat brought the house down when he shouted in the shell, "WELL, WHADDA YUH WANT??"

A Pig Tale

Poor Jane Higgins,
  She had five piggins,
And one got drowned in the Irish Sea.
  Poor Jane Higgins,
  She had four piggins,
And one flew over a sycamore tree.
  Poor Jane Higgins,
  She had three piggins,
And one was taken away for pork.
  Poor Jane Higgins,
  She had two piggins,
And one was sent to the Bishop of Cork.
  Poor Jane Higgins,
  She had one piggin,
And that was struck by a shower of hail,
  So poor Jane Higgins,
  She had no piggins,
And that's the end of my little pig tale.

James Reeves

This poem has a nursery rhyme flavour, and children respond to the words, without really understanding the meaning of *a pig tale*, *a sycamore tree*, *the Irish Sea*, or *the Bishop of Cork*. If children ask, you could explain some of the terms, after you have read the poem a few times.

The most enjoyable aspect seems to be the finger-play, culminating in a loud clap of thunder which comes just after the shower of hail (fourth last line).

Everyone holds up five fingers, and the poem begins. With each successive disaster, another finger goes down, and the children's facial expressions reflect the loss.

When you get to the line:
  and one was STRUCK by a shower of hail
you and the children clap hands as loudly as possible; then, very sadly, you relate the end of the story, while the children show their closed fists.
Perhaps, after the second-last line:
  She had no piggins
wait a moment with a sad face, then say brightly and matter-of-factly
  And that's the end of my little pig tale.

The Moo-Cow-Moo

The moo-cow-moo has a tail like rope
And it's tangled down where it grows
And it's just like feeling a piece of soap
All over the moo-cow's nose.

The moo-cow-moo has lots of fun
Just swishing her tail about.
But if she opens her mouth — I RUN
For that's where the "M O O O" comes out.

This is greatly enhanced if you ask the children to pass a piece of sloppy wet soap around the room. Get them to shut their eyes. All you need to do is to read the poem, shudder a little as you mention the *piece of soap* . . .

The climax and huge enjoyment comes in the last line. Children make an enormous *M O O O O O O!* and the teacher, pretending to be frightened, puts her hands over her ears, hides, or races out of the room (for a second or two).

This poem, and *A Pig Tale*, are ideal for Preps and younger children.

Things

Trains are for going,
Boats are for rowing,
Seeds are for sowing,
Noses for blowing,
   And sleeping's for bed.

Dogs are for pawing,
Logs are for sawing,
Crows are for cawing,
Rivers for thawing,
   And sleeping's for bed.

Flags are for flying,
Stores are for buying,
Glasses for spying,
Babies for crying,
   And sleeping's for bed.

Cows are for mooing,
Chickens for shooing,
Blue is for bluing,
Things are for doing,
   And sleeping's for bed.

Games are for playing,
Hay is for haying,
Horses for neighing,
Sayings for saying,
   And sleeping's for bed.

Money's for spending,
Patients for tending,
Branches for bending,
Poems for ending,
   And sleeping's for bed.

William Jay Smith

This is a perfect blend of activity, sometimes noisy, and peace, perfect peace.
In each verse, the final line:
   And sleeping's for bed.
must be accompanied by each child placing his hands together (prayer style) and resting his sleeping head (i.e. eyes and mouths shut) upon his hands. There must not be a murmur during this time and the short silence which follows.

   With the children work out motions for each line before the poem is presented. The ideas given here are only examples.

Verse 1:
Trains are for going,   (Speak in a choof-choofy manner)

Boats are for rowing,   (Make a rowing motion)

Seeds are for sowing,   (Scatter
                              pretend-seeds all
                              over)
Noses for blowing,   (Hold noses)
And sleeping's for bed.   (Described earlier.)

You may like to make up some verses of your
own:

    Schools are for _____
    Wood is for _____
    Churns are for _____
    Wheels are for _____
       And sleeping's for bed.

Make up your own rhymes. Children love
guessing the end word.

Mud

I like mud.
   I like it on my clothes.
I like it on my fingers,
   I like it on my toes:

Dirt's pretty ordinary
   And dust's a dud.
For a really good mess-up

   I like mud.

John Smith

    Ideally, each child could hold a small ball of
clay (from the art room) and squelch it
around in time to the beat of the poem.
On the last line:
   I like mud.
they could press their hands onto a piece of
paper as the word *mud* is read.
Make a gallery of hand mud-prints.
OR
    Try finger painting. Mix up some slimy
brown finger paint (paint mixed with paste).
Place in shallow dishes. Children work in
groups of four or five. As you read the poem,
children dabble rhythmically in the paint, and
as suggested earlier, make hand prints at the
end.

Over and Under

Bridges are for going over water,
Boats are for going over sea;
Dots are for going over dotted *i*'s,
And blankets are for going over me.

   Over and under,
    Over and under,
     Crack the whip,
      And hear the thunder.

Divers are for going under water,
Seals are for going under sea;
Fish are for going under mermaids' eyes,
And pillows are for going under me.

   Over and under,
    Over and under,
     Crack the whip,
      And hear the thunder,
       Crack-crack-crack,
        Hear the crack of thunder!

William Jay Smith

This poem is very good for developing the
concept of over and under.
Children make their own actions for the over
and under descriptions (bridges, boats, dots,
blankets . . .), but in the refrain all join
together, swinging hands or arms in time to
the words. On the word *crack*, all children
clap hands loudly. At the very end of the
poem, there will be three loud cracks followed
by an even louder one, as the poem closes:
   Hear the CRACK of thunder!

Try various other concepts: up/down, in/out,
through/between, above/below, open/shut,
top/bottom.

Feather or Fur

When you watch for
Feather or fur
Feather or fur
Do not stir
Do not stir.

Feather or fur
Come crawling
Creeping
Some come peeping
Some by night
And some by day.
Most come gently
All come softly
Do not scare
A friend away.

When you watch for
Feather or fur
Feather or fur
Do not stir
Do not stir.

John Becker

A quiet poem, spoken in a hushed voice —
almost a whisper. It is suitable for any themes
on animals, and enjoyed by most grade levels.
The poem could be read before or after
exploring round the school, looking for
feathery or furry animals.
Discuss various creatures, if you can't find the
real ones, or use pictures.

For younger grades, you or the children
could cut out shapes of cats, mice, rabbits,
emus, ducks, chooks, parrots . . . Children
then stick furry or feathery textured materials
over the shapes (cotton wool, carpet pieces,
velvet, hat feathers, old pillow feathers . . .)

For older grades, this is an excellent poem
to illustrate. Make headings and a border to
decorate the poem which will have been
written in their most beautiful calligraphy.

Bananas and Cream

Bananas and cream,
Bananas and cream,
All we could say was
Bananas and cream.

We couldn't say fruit,
We couldn't say cow;
We didn't say sugar,
We don't say it now.

Bananas and cream,
Bananas and cream,
All we could shout was
BANANAS AND CREAM.

We didn't say why,
We didn't say how;
We forgot it was fruit,
We forgot the old cow;
We never said sugar,
We only said WOW!

BANANAS AND CREAM,
BANANAS AND CREAM;
ALL THAT WE WANT IS
BANANAS AND CREAM!

We didn't say dish,
We didn't say spoon;
We said not tomorrow,
But NOW and HOW SOON.

Bananas and cream,
Bananas and cream?
We yelled for bananas,
Bananas and scream!

David McCord

We have found that one of the secrets of
success in Children's Literature is through a
child's stomach. *Bananas and Cream* has the
added advantages of being bouncy, joyful and
easily memorised.
An idea: Say to the children, "I'll bet I can

teach you to memorise a poem of thirty lines (seven verses) in fifteen minutes." Their reaction will be one of horror! shock! shriek!! but you will find that they will really enjoy the challenge.

Read the poem, then read it again, encouraging children to join in as you read, and emphasising the *scream* at the end. Allow them ten to fifteen minutes to memorise the poem, and then ask for volunteers.

If you can afford fifteen bananas and a bottle of cream, it is CERTAIN to succeed!

Car Attack

On last year's Halloween
A car hit Auntie Jean.
Unhinged by this attack,
My Auntie hit it back.

She hit it with her handbag
And knocked it with her knee.
She socked it with a sandbag
And thumped it with a tree.

On last year's Halloween
A car hit Auntie Jean.
And now, my Auntie's better
But the car is with the wrecker.

Doug MacLeod

Children have so much fun acting this poem, but it is essential to teach them the rudiments of stage performance — i.e. when Auntie Jean hits the car, she doesn't really hit it; she stops just short of the target, so that it seems that she connects. Practise this several times until the children have learned the technique.

Children work in groups. If they're working in twos, one player is Auntie Jean — the other is the car. In this way the whole class can join in the performance at the same time. Change parts — if children wish.

An idea for the last verse would be to choose two children: one to say the first three lines in a factual-formal news reader's voice, and another to deliver the last line in a carefree, throw-away manner.

On some occasions, the cars have all been known to crumple in dilapidated heaps at the end of the poem!

Cat

Cat!
Scat!
Atter her, atter her,
Sleeky flatterer,
Spitfire chatterer,
Scatter her, scatter her,
    Off her mat!
    Wuff!
    Wuff!
    Treat her rough!
Git her, git her,
Whiskery spitter!
Catch her, catch her,
Green-eyed scratcher!
    Slathery
    Slithery
    Hisser,
    Don't miss her!
Run till you're dithery,
    Hithery
    Thithery
    Pfitts! Pfitts!
    How she spits!
    Spitch! Spatch!
    Can't she scratch!
Scritching the bark
Of the sycamore*-tree,
She's reached her ark
And's hissing at me
    Pfitts! Pfitts!
    Wuff! Wuff!
    Scat,
    Cat!
    That's
    That!

Eleanor Farjeon

There are zillions of animal books full of cat poems, but this old favourite never seems to run out of puff.

The poem could be written on a large piece of material with a waterproof felt pen (just iron it when it's crumpled), or write the poem on a chart or the board.

Use different colours for various parts of the poem.

Before reading the poem together, talk about the different sounds of the poem. Discuss which children could perform different parts. Are there some parts the whole class could say? How should the following be said?

Pfitts! Pfitts!	(Spit it out)
Slathery	
Slithery	
Hisser,	(Make these very hissy ssssy
Don't miss, her!	words)
Wuff! Wuff!	(rough growls — not meek woofs)
Spitch! Spatch!	(Short sharp bursts)

Practise different methods of reading or performing the poem.

* *sycamore* It is quite acceptable to change the word *sycamore* into *eucalypt* if you wish to Australianise the poem. Eleanor Farjeon wouldn't mind!

I Never Win at Parties

I never win at parties.
I never win at all.
Someone gets the prizes.
Someone wins the ball.
Someone gets the roses
Off the birthday cake.
I don't get the roses;
I get the stomach ache.
Someone pins the tail
On the donkey's seat.
When I pin the donkey,
It ends up on his feet.
Someone drops the clothes pins

Right where they should go.
I can't hit the bottle,
Even bending low.
I do not know the reason,
Unless it's that I'm small,
Why I don't win at parties.
I just don't win at all.

Marci Ridlon

Every child will empathise with the feelings expressed in this poem. Read it in a downtrodden saddish sort of way, and you'll notice the nods of agreement and sympathy. Most children have attended parties and most have lost at one time or another.

Parties are memorable occasions for children; they don't forget the highs or the lows; and the anecdotes will flow after the poem is read. Various activities could follow. E.g. children work in groups: one the winners, the others the losers, each group speaking the appropriate lines. This could be extended into a more general discussion about good luck/bad luck, winning and losing.

Or if a party is imminent, the birthday child can be the actor whilst the whole class recites the poem, and if he becomes too downcast, perhaps you could persuade the class to give a Standing Ovation as described on page 25.

Try a few of the party games mentioned in the poem.

The Little Blue Engine

The little blue engine looked up at the hill.
His light was weak, his whistle was shrill.
He was tired and small, and the hill was tall
And his face blushed red as he softly said,
"I think I can, I think I can, I think I can."

So he started up with a chug and a strain,
And he puffed and pulled with might
    and main.
And slowly he climbed, a foot at a time,

172

And his engine coughed as he whispered
   soft,
"I think I can, I think I can, I think I can."

With a squeak and a creak and a toot
   and a sigh,
With an extra hope and an extra try,
He would not stop — now he neared
   the top —
And strong and proud he cried out loud,
"I think I can, I think I can, I think I can!"

He was almost there, when — *CRASH!*
   SMASH! BASH!
He slid down and mashed into engine hash
On the rocks below . . . which goes
   to show
If the track is tough and the hill is rough,
THINKING you can just ain't enough!

Shel Silverstein

Read the poem. Then invite discussion:- what
happened to the Little Blue Engine? Why
didn't he reach the top? This could lead to
debate about the ability to do certain things at
certain stages in order to achieve your goals. It
is senseless to be wildly unrealistic: a
ten-year-old can't run a four-minute mile, no
matter how hard he tries. (On the other hand,
if you don't have high aspirations you will
never reach the top — whether it's mountain
climbing or writing poetry — the question is
one of balance.) In the same way the Little
Blue Engine (unlike his more colourful
relation) just didn't have the puff to get to the
top.
Try various train noises (steam train *choof*
with *whistle* is effective.) One half of the grade
can repeat *I think I can* very slowly at first,
then building up to a crescendo as they reach
the top, whilst the other half choofs in rhythm.
The teacher can orchestrate the climb up the
hill and the final spectacular CRASH in which
all children participate.

Mr Tom Narrow

A scandalous man
   Was Mr. Tom Narrow,
He pushed his grandmother
   Round in a barrow.
And he called out loud
   As he rang his bell,
"Grannies to sell!
   Old grannies to sell!"

The neighbours said
   As he passed them by,
"This poor old lady
   We will not buy.
He surely must be
   A mischievous man
To try for to sell
   His own dear Gran."

"Besides," said another,
   "If you ask me,
She'd be very small use
   That I can see,"
"You're right," said a third,
   "And no mistake —
A very poor bargain
   She'd surely make."

So Mr. Tom Narrow
   He scratched his head,
And he sent his grandmother
   Back to bed;

And he rang his bell
   Through all the town
Till he sold his barrow
   For half a crown.

James Reeves

This poem leads naturally to improvisation.
For example, one group at Rosevern made
themselves into a wheel barrow into which
they hurled the poor soon-to-be-sold Grannie.
   The best idea is to read the poem right
through the first time; then allot parts and
allow children rehearsal time.

Choose various groups of neighbours, and they exclaim, in words of their own, their reactions to the sale. "What use would you have for a worn-out old Gran?" "Poor old thing — look at that dreadful man — it's disgusting!" "People like Tom Narrow should be put in gaol. We'll report him to the R.S.P.C.A."

All children will be involved, so there will be many groups of neighbours. Usually, one child in each group acts as a catalyst to develop the initial idea, until all the groups are satisfied with their contributions.

Some children might help Mr. Tom Narrow to make a FOR SALE sign, and a kind teacher will surely lend a bell.

Really, after that, you've done your bit — it's now up to the children. After several rehearsals, invite the V.P or another class to view the final production. If you intend producing the poem as a play, it helps in introducing the show to have an M.C. who presents the characters:

"And now, Ladies and Gentlemen, girls and boys, Grade 4C would like to show you their production of *Mr Tom Narrow*. Tom. (*Tom bows.*) Grannie. (*Grannie totters her bow.*) All the neighbours. (*Each group bows.*) And last, but not least, the wheelbarrow!" (*Cheer! Cheer! Cheer!*)

Menial Note: Explain *half a crown*, but if you wish to modernise the text, you could replace it with:

And he rang his bell
  Near every fence
Till he sold his barrow
  For fifty cents.

Strange Tree

Away beyond the Jarboe house
I saw a different kind of tree.
Its trunk was old and large and bent,
And I could feel it look at me.

The road was going on and on
Beyond to reach some other place.
I saw a tree that looked at me,
And yet it did not have a face.

It looked at me with all its limbs,
It looked at me with all its bark.
The yellow wrinkles on its sides
Were bent and dark.

And then I ran to get away,
But when I stopped and turned to see
The tree was bending to the side —
And leaning out to look at me.

Elizabeth Madox Roberts

One idea is to say something like this to the children: "The other night I was walking home late, and just as I turned into my street I noticed the old tree on the corner. There was something different about it. Now of course I know that trees can't *look* at you, but this one seemed really scary. It was as if it was trying to point its branches at me. I sped home!

"Now stand up and we'll try an experiment: I want each of you to make yourself into a tree. You are no longer a person — you have no face, arms, legs, body — but a trunk, branches, twigs and leaves. Feel yourself into TREENESS: project tree feelings towards me. Let me *feel* the treeness of you."

Then read the poem, walking in and out of the forest of trees. It's a good idea to memorise the poem so that you can stare at the trees and not at the book.

You will find the children will probably react to various words. E.g. when you say:

bent and dark

most of them will bend and become dark.

When you reach the last verse:
And then I ran to get away
race towards the door or hide behind a table, and as you finish the last words, and all the trees are bending towards you, utter a loud shriek or shudder.

Children may have anecdotes about spooky trees they've encountered.

For more ideas, glance at the *Day in the Grades* theme on Trees (pages 46–56).

UPPER LEVEL

The Swagman

(to John)

Green valleys for white flocks of sheep;
red deserts for black crows;
dark billabongs for light of stars . . . . .
and me for all of those.

Raggedy trees for kookaburras;
ridge-rocks for the close
of day with colours; roads for
tramping . . . . .
and me for all of those.

Rex Ingamells

After you have read the poem, discuss it with the children.
Find out if they know about swagmen.
The word *swagman* is not specifically mentioned in any of the lines, so why is the poem called *The Swagman*? What lines give you the clue or hint?
Can you remember at least six things mentioned in the poem which the Swagman loves (black crows, white flocks of sheep)?

Although short, this poem lends itself to a more formal discussion on poetic qualities such as **imagery** — *raggedy trees for kookaburras* — and **structure**: get children to tap the rhythm to the first stanza, then point out the difference in the second stanza,

particularly the end of line two which is followed straight on by the beginning of line three. If unaided, children would read
ridge rocks for the close (pause)
of day with colours; (spoken as if it is a new thought instead of reading it as a complete sentence)

Talk about the **lack of capital letters** at the start of each new line. How is **rhyme** used in this poem? (Some poems rhyme, some don't.)

Although the actual word **Dedication** was not used, this poem was dedicated (written especially for) the poet's friend, John. One of the highest honours you can receive is to have a book or poem dedicated to you. It is a writer's special way of saying thank-you for all your help, love and friendship. Watch out for dedications in other books.

Further activities
Now that you have discussed imagery with children, ask them to make up some images of their own. Perhaps you could start them off with some beginnings or ends:
E.g. grey eucalypts for_____
dusty tracks for_____
_____for flapping wings.
_____for echoing calls.
Write your own poem along the same lines, perhaps about the city:

The City Slicker

Grey cities for loud cries and noise;
orange lights for T.V. shows,
blaring sirens — danger looms . . .
and me for all of those.

Dark sky-scrapers for scratching sky;
bulldozers for crashing blows;
Footpaths deep in paper leaves . . .
and me for all of those.

All About Boys and Girls

I know all about boys, I do,
And I know all about little girls, too.
I know what they eat. I know what
   they drink.
I know what they like. I know what
   they think.

And so I'm writing this to say,
Don't let children out to play.
It makes them sad. They'd rather go
To school or to the dentist. Oh,

I know they're bashful about saying
How much it hurts to be out playing
When they could go to school and spell
And mind their manners. They won't tell

How tired they are of games and toys.
But I know girls, and I know boys.
They like to sweep floors, chop the wood,
And practise being very good.

They'd rather sit and study hard
Than waste the whole day in the yard.
What good is fun and making noise?
That's not for girls! That's not for boys!

John Ciardi

Copy the poem on board and cover it with a chart, picture or map. Read poem in a self-righteous didactic tone, perhaps allowing a slight smirk to appear now and then — or a twinkle in the eye.

Is the poet right? Does he *really* know all about boys and girls? Does he know *anything* about boys and girls? Read the poem again and ask the children to indicate with a TOOT TOOT when he's wrong, and a CHEER when he is right.

Uncover the poem and make a list of the things the poet believes that boys and girls like. You should be able to list ten things.

Say to the children: Now it's *your* turn to pay the poet back.

Tell him what you think about adults. Make up a few verses which begin:
I know all about teachers, I do,
   and I know all about parents, too. . .
Or, if you have a particularly inventive grade, you could begin:
I know all about poets, I do,
   And I know all about writers, too. . .

Make some whole class or individual lists, using classifications such as these:

Things I like to eat	Things I hate to eat
Games or things I like to play	Games or things I hate to play
T.V. shows I like	T.V. shows I hate
Words I like to hear	Words I hate to hear
Places I like to go	Places I hate to go

If this is a whole class list, write the children's ideas up on the board. Discuss. Then children write their own versions in their books. If it is to be an individual task, run a sheet off on the duplicator and children work quietly after a brief discussion.

Write a letter to Mr. Ciardi, pointing out the error of his ways.

Make a class book in which each child draws a page, with a message thereon. Title of book:
   I know John Ciardi, I do. . .

The Bogeyman

In the desolate depths of a perilous
   place
the bogeyman lurks, with a snarl
   on his face.
Never dare, ,never dare to approach his
   dark lair

for he's waiting . . . just waiting . . .
  to get you.

He skulks in the shadows, relentless
  and wild
in his search for a tender, delectable
  child.
With his steely sharp claws and his
  slavering jaws
oh he's waiting . . . just waiting . . .
  to get you.

Many have entered his dreary domain
but not even one has been heard
  from again.
They no doubt made a feast for the
  butchering beast
and he's waiting . . . just waiting . . .
  to get you.

In that sulphurous, sunless and
  sinister place
he'll crumple your bones in his bogey
  embrace.
Never never go near if you hold you life
  dear,
for oh! . . . what he'll do . . .
  when he gets you!

Jack Prelutsky

Write the poem on board or material. Read the whole poem quietly, eerily whispering the last line of each stanza.

If possible, read in a darkened room — the film room or the dark room, and show the poem on an overhead transparency or chart. You read the first three lines of each verse, children whisper the fourth.

At the end, when he gets you, make a long, drawn-out, shrieky

    o

   o o

y   *u*

      u uuuuuuuuuu!

Look at the literary devices the poet uses: how does he achieve a spooky effect? Discuss **alliteration**, e.g.

> *He skulks in the shadows, relentless*
>
> or
>
> *In that sulphurous, sunless and*
> *sinister place.*

Repetition is effectively used: the children expect to hear the same line at the end of each verse, therefore the last line of the poem achieves its deadly impact if it is spoken extremely dramatically. Ask children to try some alliterations of their own. Collect and compare. Topics can be chosen by teacher or students. Some ideas: walking down a dark lane, a quicksand swamp at midnight, groping around during an impenetrable fog.

Finish off by reading the poem again, or by telling or reading a short ghost story.
Try *Watch Out for Witches* by Ridsdale and Ferguson, (Nelson), and *Frights on Dark Nights* by Ferguson & Park (McGraw Hill)

Rafferty Rides Again

There's a road outback that becomes a track
Where the hills dip down to the plain,
And on misty moonlight nights up there
The old inhabitants all declare
On his big black stallion (or was it a mare?)
  Rafferty rides again.

A bushranger bold in the days of old,
'Twas an evil name that he bore,
Till they shot him down from behind a
  tree —
At least that's the yarn they told to me
When I asked who this Rafferty bloke
  might be,
  And what he was riding for.

And it now appears, after all the years
That low in his grave he has lain,
That over the hills, in the same old way,
Dashing and debonair, reckless, gay,
On his chestnut charger (or was it a bay?)
  Rafferty rides again.

I have waited long the old hills among,
But my vigils have been in vain;
I've perched all night in a towering tree,
But devil a ride he'd ride for me,
Though I would have given the world to
    see
    Rafferty ride again.

But the tale is true that I'm telling you,
Though it's ages since he was slain;
To all the folk in the hills 'tis known
That, awesome and spectral, and all
    alone,
On his snow-white courser (or was it a
    roan?)
    Rafferty rides again.

Thomas V. Tierney

Of all the poetic forms, the one which seems to appeal most of all to Australians is the Ballad. (Paterson, Lawson, Gordon, and aeons of others.)

This poem has all of a ballad's qualities: it tells a good story, there is a rhyming and rhythmic stucture, and it has a repetitive refrain.

In the olden days, ballads were passed down by word of mouth, and naturally each generation told it in a slightly different way. If the character was interesting, strong or romantic enough, the story of his life would be passed on over hundreds of years — and that's how legends began.

The poet in this story is not really certain about Rafferty, but he is fascinated by the story. Obviously the part which appeals to him, and which fascinates all the students, is the mystery which surrounds the man, his life, his death and the fact that his ghost still rides alone in the old hills between the towering trees. What really happened? Why is it that the poet doesn't seem to be able to make up his mind about the kind of horse Rafferty rides:

— *big black stallion (or was it a mare?)*
— *on his chestnut charger (or was it a bay?)*

— *on his snow-white courser (or was it a roan?)*

The children will discuss the story at length. Look at the language the poet uses. He doesn't fling any old word down on the page. In poems which one remembers, vivid words are used and remembered, even if you've never seen them before —

spectral (like a ghost)
debonair (handsome, cool, dashing)

Researchers tell us that once a child uses a word, particularly in some written form, he has it for ever.

The way you treat this poem will depend on your grade. On several occasions, all that we've done is to read the poem through a couple of times, encouraging the children to join in, particularly the final line:

Rafferty rides again

in an eerie, outback Aussie echo.

How to Treat the House-plants

All she ever thinks about are
    house-plants.
She talks to them and tends them every
    day.
And she says, 'Don't hurt their feelings.
    Give them
Love. In all your dealings with them,
Treat them in a tender, *human* way.'

'Certainly, my dear,' he says. 'O.K.
Human, eh?'

But the house-plants do not seem to
    want to play.

They are stooping, they are drooping,
They are kneeling in their clay:
They are flaking, they are moulting,
Turning yellow, turning grey,
And they look . . . well, quite revolting
As they sigh, and fade away.

So after she has left the house he gets
    them

And he sets them in a line against the
   wall,
And I cannot say in cossets them or pets
   them —
No, he doesn't sympathize with them all.
Is he tender? Is he human? Not a bit.
No, to each of them in turn he says:
   'You *twit*!

You're a
   Rotten little skiver,
   Cost a fiver,
   Earn your keep!

You're a
   Dirty little drop-out!
   You're a cop-out!
   You're a creep!

You're a
   Mangy little whinger!
   You're a cringer!
   Son, it's true —

   I have justbin
   To the dustbin
   Where there's *better men than you*!

   Get that stem back!

   Pull your weight!

   Stick you leaves out!

   STAND UP STRAIGHT!'

And, strange to say, the plants
   co-operate.
So when she comes back home and
   finds them glowing,
Green and healthy, every one a king,
She says, 'It's *tenderness* that gets them
   growing!
How strange, the change a little *love* can
   bring!'

'Oh yes,' he says. 'Not half. Right. Love's
   the thing.'

Kit Wright

This poem is pure fun.
Involve the children right from the beginning:
"We 're going to act this poem, but just to give
you some idea, I'll read it the first time, then
we'll audition for parts."
Read poem.
   "Who would like to be the flower-loving
lady?" Choose someone who must
demonstrate his or her skill by kissing the
leaves of the classroom's pot plants. We say
his or her because many of our extrovert
Grade 5 males love this part.
   Audition for flower-hating husbands.
Because we want to involve more children, we
usually split the husband's lines into several
parts. All the other class members become the
plants: sitting in their seats. NO TALKING —
plants do not talk! They fade away as
requested by the poet. When the husband
turns on them in anger, they gradually come
back to life.
By the time the wife returns, all the plants are
quietly blooming and glowing as she says:
   "It's tenderness that gets them growing
      How strange the change a little love can
   bring!"
To which the long-suffering husband replies,
with a sigh,
   "Oh yes . . . Not half. Right. Love's the
   thing!"
This poem always works — whether acted or
not — but timing and practice are essential if
it is to become a memorable production.

Silent Hill

Anne says she dreams sometimes — and
   so do I
About the child we saw go by.
In the late afternoon we saw her pass,
Slowly and without a sound. The deep
   grass
Bent before her, as where a soft wind
   goes.
Except we know that no wind ever blows
The dark deep grass on Silent Hill.

179

My grandma says that back before her
    day,
There was a fine house there upon the
    crest
Where now a blackened chimney leans
    to rest
Against the sky. And now and then
    nearby,
Like a leaf of ash, a dark bird drifts
    without a cry.
Nothing else goes there. No boys climb
    up to play.
Even the wild deer seem to keep away.
But Anne is not afraid. And sometimes
    we go near
To listen to the soft hush, deep as fear,
Heavy as smoke, that seems to hang
    there still,
Where only dreams walk now — on
    silent hill.

Anne says she dreams sometimes — and
    so do I —
About the child we saw go by,
On Silent Hill.

Zilpha Keatley Snyder

This is a quiet and contemplative poem. All
that may be needed is to read it once or twice,
and allow the children to think and to
daydream (without talking).
Leave it at that, if it seems appropriate.

We add these further ideas for those who wish
to continue with activities.
    The poem must be read in absolute silence.
Pause before you begin and wait when you
have finished reading. Many teachers are
embarrassed by the silence which follows an
excellent story or poem. While children are still
basking in their recent literary adventure, the
teacher claps her hands and says brightly:
"Now then! Stand up! Make yourself into a
hill!" Or worse still, "Hands up those who
liked this poem?" Our very strong advice is

NEVER SAY THIS LINE! It is completely
unnecessary. You will be able to tell if the
children really enjoyed it, by the looks on their
faces. Also, how many children would be game
enough to say, "No, I hated it, Sir"?

Things to note about the poem

Similes and metaphors:
> *like a leaf of ash*
> *heavy as smoke*
> *deep as fear*

The haunting refrain:
On Silent Hill.

Questions to think about:

• Have you ever been somewhere in the
country — all alone — so quiet, so still, it
seems as if even the wind doesn't blow?
• Who is Anne? Who is the mysterious child?
Why is Anne not afraid when others are?
• Why is there something to fear on Silent
Hill?
• Why does no one go there — no animals,
no boys?
• What does *Where only dreams walk now*
mean?
• How do you *listen to the soft hush?*

Illustration

The poem would be very good to illustrate:
> *a blackened chimney leans to rest*
> *Against the sky.*

Similes

Try some similes of your own:
• like a mist drifting over the hill
• as bronze stone
• like a burning fireball the sun clashed with
the sky

Model some phrases on *deep as fear*:
> grand as_____
> fearful as_____
> silent as_____
> gentle as_____
> grumpy as_____

6 Emergency Teaching

Getting a Job and Getting Invited Back

Emergency or relief teaching is a very unpredictable occupation. You never know when the call will come, but you can bet that on the very day you have planned something else, the phone will ring. To ensure a steady stream (or trickle!) of work you *can* take some initiatives which will help.

181

Before You Begin

To encourage an invitation to teach, nothing beats personal contact. The school will probably have your name and address on a centrally distributed master list, but most schools compile a short list of reliables whom they phone first. A personal visit by you, giving details about your specialist areas, grade preferences and availability, might mean the addition of your name to the list.

When you are starting out it is wise to try to meet as many requests to teach as possible. By so doing you can look over a wide range of schools and decide which would suit you best. Tell schools if you enjoyed working there — it will encourage them to invite you back. On the other hand, if you found a particular school unsuitable, let them know. If you suggest that it is inconvenient to work there, it will save the school making futile phone calls to you in the future, and you won't have to make up phoney excuses.

If you have been emergency teaching for a number of years, it is a good idea to contact the school at the start of the year to let them know you are still available. Tell them also if you are holidaying or are unavailable for an extended period. Schools record days when relief teachers work and when they are unavailable. When you return from your holiday, let them know. You don't want them to forget you.

What the School Expects of You

It is not common for the red carpet to be dragged out for the emergency teacher. You usually arrive at school-time peak hour. Everyone is hustling. You often feel like excess baggage. No one has time to spoon feed you. Above all, the reliever who is appreciated the most is the one who takes over the grade with the minimum of fuss. The schools expect the reliever to put in a solid day's work and show genuine concern for the children.

As well, there are certain common procedures which most schools require of their emergency teachers.

* Before going to the classroom, contact the Principal or Deputy Principal, even though you may be familiar with the school.
* Punctuality is important. You should be at school by 8.45 a.m. if you have been notified before 8.00 a.m.
  (Of course there will be times when the school has not been able to contact you until nearly 9 o'clock, and in such a case they will arrange for someone else to look after the class until you arrive.)
* Teach rather than supervise. Try to follow the work progam. Adapt and modify; use your own ideas and expertise, but try to cover the subject areas specified.
* Leave a record of what has been taught and what, if anything, has been substituted.
* Do your duty! But beware. Do not do everyone's duty. Reasonable requests should be accepted.

* Accept the same responsibility for the grade as the class teacher. Accompany the grade to the specialist programs where required, supervise lunch eating, make sure that the room is left clean and tidy.
* Use common sense in following normal classroom procedures. As a general rule, don't make changes in the classroom. Ask the teacher next door if the cash collection procedure is confusing. If the system for taking readers home is complicated, postpone it for a day.

   Maintain a high standard of professional ethics. Don't compare one school with another, one teacher with another.

What you can Expect from the School

* Ideally, schools will notify you early as to the day or days required, and grades to be taught. Often you will be told at this point

about any special programs such as excursions, sports days, etc.
* Relieving teachers *are* welcomed by school staffs, although some schools have strange ways of showing it. Generally by morning tea, staff have time to chat. Wholesale introductions are embarrassing, but ask if you have not met grade co-ordinators, and the teachers from the rooms next door.

* You should be provided by the school with the following organisational details:
   hours of duty
   recess and dismissal times
   yard duty times
   wet day procedures
   lunch routines
   important school rules
   details about team teaching, streaming, etc.
   plan of school (emergency fire exits, etc.)

This information is usually outlined in a school handbook or folder and is available from the Principal or Secretary.

If you have the time and interest the school will also provide you with school policy documents and courses relevant to the grade you are teaching.

* To enable you to function efficiently in the classroom, the class teacher should leave:

> the Grade Roll
> the Grade time-table
> the work program, together with any guides, books, sheets, supplies, and other necessary instructional materials
> details about special programs, library, art, phys. ed, broadcasts, regular activities
> essential information about reading groups, research groups, gifted programs, team teaching, parental involvement.

How to get Invited Back

The most sought-after emergency teachers are those who really will help out in an emergency. There may be a hundred good reasons why you can't come on a cold wet Monday, and of course all your experience has been in Preps, but the person who says "Yes" to the desperate 8.47 a.m. call for that errant Grade 5/6 lives long in the memory of the Principal. If you accept the difficult grade and manage them well, you will be constantly in demand. But beware! Your reputation will spread like wildfire. You will be inundated with calls for tough jobs. Make sure you let the Principal know where your preference lies.

To increase your popularity rating and therefore enhance your chances of further work you might also:

* Write a brief note to the class teacher you replaced letting her know

> the areas covered during the day
> what still needs to be done
> details about work corrected.

* Leave examples of activities completed. (The teacher will love it if you arrange a display of art or written language.)
* If the teacher you have replaced has a free period, you might like to offer your services elsewhere. This is always appreciated.

To Prevent Emergencies —Be Prepared

Now and then you will be asked to replace a teacher who has left you with no material or guidance for the day's program. On these occasions when time and resources are sparse and the nine o'clock onslaught is imminent, emergency procedures are required.

1 Before School Begins: Write Yourself a Note

Plan the day's work in chronological order. Think of the day in chunks — before play, before lunch, after lunch, etc. If you can't find the teacher's work program, there is usually a timetable somewhere around the room. Slot sheets, reading materials, poems, spelling, maths, phys. ed. into the plan. Take note of the specialists' times and underline them in black.

Before play
Collect excursion money
News
Fast Maths: Number patterns.
Poem: Car Attack by Doug McLeod

After play   Continue Project Work
Group 1 – Dragons
       2 – Wasps (with Mrs Baker)
       3 – Lizards (with me)
Maths Spatial Relations
       (Measurement in Maths p.15–17)
Library   11.30 – 12.15

After lunch   Word Play Sheet 6 from
              Emergency
Reading Group 1 – with me
       Y.A.R 12 p.67
       Y.A.R Activity 12
Spelling   Hangman's Noose

After play   Written Language Because–
Sheet 9
Art with Mrs Parslow
     Take along face masks.

The day's work might be entirely different from your note, or you might manage only half the activities you planned, but it is very comforting to discover at 11.35 that you have not run out of things to do.

2 When School Starts: Utilise the Early Morning Breather

In most grades there is some kind of discussion time first thing in the morning. Use *Show and Tell* or *Morning Talk* to gather your thoughts and get things organised. *U.S.S.R.* (Uninterrupted Sustained Silent Reading), described on page 32, is also an excellent early morning activity and will provide you with another twenty or thirty minutes in which to plan and prepare.

3 During the Day: Seek Help

When desperate, ask. In most schools a number of people are resource persons. The teacher-librarian has access to most of the school's materials and is usually pleased to help — that's her job. If the school employs a Special Resource Teacher, she too can provide invaluable advice and assistance.

In the senior grades there is invariably a clutch of children who act as monitors or assistants. They will only be too happy to tell you where materials are and how the classroom normally operates.

4 Working Equipment: The Bag of Tricks

By far the best means of coping with those times when you are called at the last moment to teach *that* notorious grade, whose teacher only leaves you with an empty chalk box and a dried up bottle of clag, is to build up a collection of essential items at home, and select from these prior to the day's teaching. Included in your bag of tricks might be:
Manilla folders itemised according to grades and subjects. Whenever you use a sheet or an idea which works well in a particular grade, keep an example and file it.
A cassette of songs

Entertainment and diversionary activities

Depending on your personality, these may include a magician's bag of tricks, miming cards (see pages 11–13), a guitar, xylophone or recorder, pictures, photos or slides . .

Books

Always keep on hand your favourite books for each grade. See Chapter 5 for books, stories and poems. As well, there are dozens of excellent books which include zingy ideas for any grade. The criteria for selecting these books are i easily applicable ideas

ii activities which cover all grades from Preps to Grade 6.

Consider some of the following titles:

* The *Getting Started* Series (Port Phillip Press)
* *Guidelines in Number* Levels 1–5, and following (Education Department of Victoria)
* *Listening, Creating and Moving* — Leask and Lucas (Drummond).
* *Mathematics Curriculum Guides / Measurement* (Education Department of Victoria)
* *New Games* (Department of Youth, Sport and Recreation)
* *Spelling: A Teachers' Guide* — Hudson (Landmark)
* *Twenty Tiny Text Books — Creative Writing in a Matchbox* — Ferguson (Hodja)

You don't need to supply everything for the grade, but you might need these in an emergency — and when you do get your own grade, all these materials will be really useful.

Goodbye and Good Luck!

Index